Borderless Kingdom

Living Without Limits in God's Authority

Dr. Peter Bonadie

Copyright © 2025 Peter Bonadie Worldwide

All rights reserved. No part of this book may be reproduced, stored in a retrieval system, or transmitted in any form or by any means, electronic, mechanical, photocopy, recording, or otherwise, without the prior written permission of the publisher, except for brief quotations used in reviews or scholarly works.

For permissions, contact:

Peter Bonadie Worldwide

🌐 www.peterbonadieworldwide.com

Dedication

To every dreamer who was told to *stay in your lane*. To every visionary who saw beyond the limits of the systems around them. To the misfits, the wanderers, the pioneers, and the prophets who refused to be confined by religion, culture, geography, or fear. To those who were measured, labeled, and restricted, yet never stopped believing that there was more.

This book is for you. You are living proof that the *Kingdom of God* knows no borders, no ceilings, and offers no apologies. May your life resonate with the sound of heaven's expansion, and may you walk boldly through every wall the world tries to place in your path.

You were never meant to live behind walls. You were born to live borderless.

Acknowledgment

First and foremost, I give glory to the Sovereign King, *Jesus Christ*, whose Kingdom knows no end and whose Spirit knows no boundaries. Thank You for the divine revelation, inspiration, and limitless grace to write these words. Every chapter is a whisper of Your eternal voice echoing through time.

To the Holy Spirit, my ever-present teacher, guide, and power source, you are the true Author behind these pages. Thank You for opening the eyes of my understanding to dimensions far beyond intellect and for stirring in me a vision of a *Kingdom without walls*.

To those Kingdom forerunners, teachers, and prophetic voices who dared to challenge limitations and model faith without borders, your lives have become landmarks for mine. Thank You for walking ahead so others like me could run.

To my spiritual family and ministry partners, your prayers, support, and hunger for truth have been a continual push forward. You are living proof that the borderless life is possible and active in our generation.

To every reader of this book, thank You for daring to explore the depths of what God has placed within you. It is my prayer that something written here will awaken the divine in you, break down man-made limitations, and release you into your fullest assignment.

Lastly, to that special friend who inspired me to see life through a wider lens, whose encouragement stirred the birthing of this message, your influence is forever etched in the DNA of this work.

This book is more than mine. It is a collective shout into the spirit realm declaring, *The Kingdom is here, and it will not be measured.*

Foreword

There comes a time in the history of the Church when God disrupts our comfort zones, dismantles our man-made boundaries, and invites us to rediscover the raw, wild, and limitless nature of His Kingdom. That time is now. *Borderless Kingdom* is a clarion call, a trumpet blast to a generation that has been measured, boxed in, and told how far they can go.

When I first encountered the message within this book, I felt the unmistakable wind of the Spirit blowing through every chapter. This is not just another theological treatise. This is a revelation, a spiritual blueprint that tears down the walls of religious tradition and invites the reader into a realm where faith operates without fences, where destiny unfolds without delay, and where identity is rooted not in systems, but in the sovereignty of God.

Peter Bonadie has masterfully woven together Scripture, prophetic insight, and divine imagination to paint a picture of a Kingdom that cannot be contained. He writes as one who has walked through walls, challenged limitations, and tasted the expanse of God's purpose. His words are not hypothetical; they are forged from the fires of experience and sharpened by revelation.

This book will challenge you. It will confront every small thought, every inherited limitation, and every lie that told you, "This is as far as you will ever go." It will stir the deep places within you and awaken dreams you buried long ago. But more than that, it will equip you with truth, with faith, and with the spiritual language necessary to navigate the vast territory of God's purpose for your life.

In *Borderless Kingdom*, you will find:
• A prophetic dismantling of fear-based boundaries
• A vision for apostolic expansion without constraint
• A revelation of identity that mirrors the nature of God
• A roadmap for living boldly in a world that still builds walls

To every leader, intercessor, visionary, and believer who knows deep down that there is more, this book is for you. It is a key to the next dimension. It is fuel for the fire. It is permission to break the tape and run free.

Read it slowly. Read it prayerfully. Read it prophetically.

Then step out and live borderless.

Dr. Stephen Andrews

Senior Leader, Kingdom Advancement Global

Author of *Apostolic Dimensions* and *Spirit Over Systems*

Contents

Dedication .... *III*

Acknowledgment .... *IV*

Foreword .... *VI*

Introduction .... *XI*

Chapter 1: The End Of Measuring Lines 3

Chapter 2: The Weakness Of Man-Made Walls 13

Chapter 3: The Power Of Faith In A Wall-Less World 25

Chapter 4: A City Without Fear 35

Chapter 5: The Glory Within Her 45

Chapter 6: Borderless Worship 57

Chapter 7: Borderless Identity 69

Chapter 8: Apostolic Expansion: No Borders, Just Territory 81

Chapter 9: The Fire On The Borders 93

Chapter 10: The Church Without Borders 101

Chapter 11: The Sound That Produces Uncommon Results 113

Chapter 12: The Unlimited Concept Of The Googleplex: 125

Chapter 13: The Spirit Of Limitlessness 133

Chapter 14 Unlocking The Dynamics Of Subatomic Faith 143

Chapter 15: Collapsing The Wave Function: Decision As Destiny 169

Chapter 16: 55 Scriptures On Borderless Living 191

Chapter 17: My Forty Borderless Decrees 203

Chapter 18: A 7-Day Borderless Devotional 211

Conclusion 221

Appendices 225

Introduction

A Kingdom Without Borders

In *Zechariah 2:1–5*, a prophetic image unfolds: a man holding a measuring line in his hand, prepared to define the city of Jerusalem by earthly dimensions. He intends to determine its boundaries, establish its limits, and calculate its size. But before his task can be completed, he is interrupted by the voice of God through another angel.

The Lord declares that Jerusalem will be *a city without walls because of the multitude of people and livestock in it,* and that He Himself will be *a wall of fire around her* and *the glory within her.*

This vision holds profound implications, not only for the historical Jerusalem but for every believer and for the Church at large. It is a divine announcement that God's Kingdom is not confined to human measurement. It cannot be walled in by tradition, doctrine, culture, or fear. Where men see limitation, God envisions expansion. Where humans draw lines, God erases them. He builds a city that defies containment and invites people to live in divine security, supernatural abundance, and radiant glory, without borders.

The concept of a *borderless Kingdom* is both inspiring and intimidating. For some, it conjures freedom, unlimited potential, and divine presence. For others, it may feel disorienting. We are used to walls. We build them for safety, order, and identity. Walls define where things begin and end. They separate, protect, restrict, and categorize.

Yet the Kingdom of God defies this framework. It is not designed to fit inside neatly constructed systems of men. It is not confined by geography, denomination, nationality, language, or logic. It is an ever-expanding realm ruled by an infinite King who desires to fill all things with Himself.

In this book, we will explore what it means to live in this borderless Kingdom. We will examine the habits, beliefs, and systems that seek to limit the move of God in our lives, and we will discover how the Spirit calls us beyond the boundaries of the familiar. The vision of Zechariah calls us to leave behind our measuring lines; the mental, emotional, and religious tools we use to define our spiritual journey, and embrace the vastness of what God has in store.

At the heart of this borderless Kingdom is a divine paradox: it is without walls, yet not without protection. God promises to be *a wall of fire around* His people. This is not the kind of barrier that restricts or repels; it is one that guards, empowers, and surrounds with supernatural energy. It suggests movement, passion, and divine presence. Unlike cold, hard walls of stone, the fire of God is dynamic. It cannot be breached, and it cannot be manipulated. It is alive, intentional, and powerful.

To live in a borderless Kingdom is to live surrounded not by fear, but by fire. It is to live exposed to the world, yet enclosed by heaven. This way of life demands a shift in mindset. Instead of trusting in visible safeguards; titles, buildings, credentials, denominations, bank accounts, we are invited to trust the invisible presence of the Lord. We are called to step into an open city, one where God, not man, defines the boundaries. One where our faith is not confined by religion, our identity is not boxed in by race or culture, and our hope is not limited by circumstance.

The world we live in is obsessed with lines. Political borders divide nations. Social boundaries define who belongs and who does not. Economic lines separate the privileged from the marginalized. Even the modern church often reinforces invisible walls between clergy and laity, traditional and contemporary, conservative and charismatic. But the Gospel of the Kingdom cuts through every line. It announces the arrival of a new realm where walls are irrelevant and access is granted by faith, not pedigree.

When Jesus came preaching the Kingdom of God, He was not offering a new religion. He was unveiling a new reality. His ministry constantly broke the rules: healing on the Sabbath, speaking with Samaritans, touching lepers, forgiving sinners. He stepped over every boundary that society and religion had erected. He modeled a borderless life, one where compassion crossed cultural lines and power flowed beyond ceremonial restrictions. His death tore the veil in the temple, the final symbolic wall between God and man, declaring once and for all that the Kingdom is open to all who believe.

This is the legacy of the borderless Kingdom. It is not merely a theological concept; it is a call to action. God is raising people who will move beyond comfort zones, challenge norms, and embrace divine disruption. He is calling believers who carry fire instead of fear, who walk by faith instead of sight, and who live with unshakable confidence that His glory is enough.

If you are tired of limited living, tired of being boxed in by fear, tradition, or other people's opinions, this book is for you. If you sense there is more to the Christian life than attending church, playing it safe, and following a checklist, then you are ready to explore the dimensions of a Kingdom with no walls. If you feel called to expand, pioneer, and carry the presence of God into places religion will not go, then welcome to the borderless Kingdom.

Each chapter of this book is designed to challenge your assumptions, ignite your faith, and release you into new realms of purpose. We will deal with the dangers of the "measuring line mentality," the myth of safety through walls, the power of faith to walk into the unknown, and the promise of divine fire as our only defense. We will uncover the glory that resides within us, the unstoppable nature of worship, and the rise of a church that cannot be caged.

This journey will not be easy. Living without borders requires courage. It means letting go of small thinking, religious pride, and comfort-based Christianity. It means being misunderstood, misrepresented, and even opposed. But it also means seeing God move in ways you never imagined. It means stepping into divine flow, experiencing supernatural protection, and becoming a vessel of His presence in a world full of walls.

Let this book serve as your invitation and your blueprint. The Lord is calling His people out of measured places and into multiplied spaces. He is building a city not with human hands, but by His Spirit. A city with no walls, no gates, and no limits; only glory, fire, and faith. This is the borderless Kingdom.

Are you ready to stop measuring and start moving?

Then step beyond the line. The fire is waiting. The glory is rising. And the Kingdom is advancing, without borders.

***Zechariah 2:1–5** (MSG)*
I looked up and was surprised to see a man holding a tape measure in his hand.
I said, "What are you up to?"
He said, "I am on my way to survey Jerusalem, to measure its width and length."
Just then the Messenger Angel, on his way out, met another angel coming in and said,
"Run, tell the Surveyor, 'Jerusalem will burst its walls, bursting with people, bursting with animals. And I will be right there with her,' God's Decree. 'I will be a wall of fire around unwalled Jerusalem and a radiant presence within.'"

***

***Zechariah 2:1–6** (NIV)*
Then I looked up, and there before me was a man with a measuring line in his hand.
I asked, "Where are you going?"
He answered me, "To measure Jerusalem, to find out how wide and how long it is."
Then the angel who was speaking to me left, and

*another angel came to meet him and said to him:
"Run, tell that young man, 'Jerusalem will be a city
without walls because of the great number of men and
livestock in it. And I myself will be a wall of fire around
it,' declares the Lord, 'and I will be its glory within.'"
"Come, come! Flee from the land of the north," declares
the Lord, "for I have scattered you to the four winds of
heaven," declares the Lord.*

Chapter 1

The End of Measuring Lines

In Zechariah's vision, a man appears carrying a measuring line, a tool of precision, order, and boundary. He moves with intent to measure the city of Jerusalem, to assess its dimensions and assign it physical limits. It seems like a noble endeavor on the surface. Measuring appears harmless, even helpful. After all, how can one build or protect without knowing the size of the thing in question?

But before he can complete his task, God intervenes. He sends another messenger to halt the effort. Why? Because what God was doing in Jerusalem could not, and should not, be measured. The city God envisioned was destined to be so vast, so full, so gloriously inhabited, that measuring it would be an act of limitation.

God refused to allow human hands to define divine territory.

This was the moment when heaven rejected human control. It was a decisive interruption to the natural tendency of mankind to box things in, particularly the things of God. The man with the measuring line represents more than an individual; he represents a mindset. He reflects a way of thinking that tries to contain, predict, and define what God is doing before it even unfolds. But God stepped in to stop it, because His plans are always bigger than our tape measures.

We live in a world addicted to measurement. From childhood, we are taught to measure everything: our height, our grades, our worth, our beauty, our success. We are ranked, categorized, and boxed. Churches do the same. Ministries are evaluated by attendance, tithing, square footage, and social media engagement. The temptation to measure is rooted in our desire to feel in control. We believe that if we can measure something, we can master it. But the Kingdom of God laughs at our spreadsheets.

The divine realm operates by faith, not figures. It moves by Spirit, not statistics. When we rely too heavily on human measurements, we begin to resist the very expansion God wants to bring. Measuring lines in the hands of men often become leashes that tether God's move to human comfort zones. They create an illusion of order while suffocating the unpredictable wonder of the supernatural.

God's interruption of the measuring line reveals a critical truth: there are moments when measuring is not just unnecessary, it is disobedient. There are seasons when trying to define what God is doing becomes an act of rebellion against divine creativity. When you measure something too early, you often misinterpret its purpose. The man in Zechariah's vision was prepared to build walls around a city that had not yet expanded. He was planning for a version of Jerusalem far smaller than the one God had in mind. And in doing so, he risked making the future a prisoner of the past.

We must be honest: measuring is comforting. It gives us the illusion of predictability. It allows us to plan and pace ourselves. But comfort is the enemy of calling. Faith does not thrive in environments where everything is counted and calculated. The disciples who followed Jesus had no blueprint, no GPS, no strategic plan. All they had was His voice: *Follow me.* And they followed. Where? Into the unknown. Why? Because faith thrives in environments where measurement fails.

To walk in the borderless Kingdom is to throw away the ruler. It is to surrender the need to know the outcome before you obey. It is to build without blueprints, to trust without evidence, to move when logic says, *stand still.* Every revival in history began when someone decided to obey without measuring. The moment you demand a full calculation before saying yes is the moment you forfeit divine surprises.

The measuring line mindset is the greatest enemy of enlargement. It causes believers to shrink their prayers, delay their obedience, and settle for smaller dreams. Measuring tells you to wait until you have enough money, followers, degrees, or experience. But the Kingdom does not wait for you to feel ready. It only asks if you are willing.

God told Abraham to leave everything familiar and go *to a land I will show you.* He did not give him a map, a contract, or a measuring line. He gave him a promise. And Abraham went. He became the father of faith not because he had all the answers, but because he moved beyond the boundaries of human knowledge. He abandoned the measuring mentality and embraced a mindset of trust.

When we think of measuring, we must also consider how often we measure ourselves. We look at our weaknesses, our past, our age, our limitations, and conclude that we are too small to be used by God. We use measuring lines to disqualify ourselves. But the Kingdom does not operate by the same metrics. God chose a stuttering Moses, a fearful Gideon, a shepherd boy named David, and an unwed teenager named Mary. Every one of them looked unqualified by human standards. But they were willing. And willingness always outmeasures worthiness.

In your life, what are you still trying to measure? Are you trying to measure whether your business idea is big enough to be worth the risk? Are you trying to calculate whether your ministry is successful enough to keep going? Are you waiting for the numbers to add up before you obey what God already told you? Throw away the line. Trust the voice.

Many believers operate with a safe obedience mindset. They are willing to step out, but only when the conditions are ideal. They want to walk on water, but only if the sea is calm. They want to launch ministries, but only if the finances are guaranteed. They want to move in the supernatural, but only if their reputation will not suffer. This is measured faith, and it produces measured fruit. The borderless Kingdom requires unmeasured obedience.

Even churches fall into the trap of measuring revival. They organize the Holy Spirit into time slots, budgets, and meeting agendas. But revival cannot be managed. It must be stewarded, not scripted. The early church in Acts grew not by programs but by presence. They had no measuring line. What they had was unity, hunger, and the raw fire of God. And that was enough to shake the world.

The Pharisees were expert measurers. They could quote every law, count every tithe, and dissect every doctrine. Yet when the Kingdom stood in front of them in the form of Jesus Christ, they missed it. Why? Because they measured righteousness by outward performance, not inward transformation. The measuring line made them blind. And it will do the same to us if we are not careful.

The man in Zechariah's vision represents our inner instinct to reduce God's promises to our personal logic. But God answers this instinct with a radical alternative: *Jerusalem shall be inhabited as a town without walls.* In other words, do not shrink your vision. Do not limit your expectations. Do not plan small because you are afraid of failure. Plan big because God is involved. Think borderless because you serve a God without boundaries.

It is time to take a prophetic inventory. Where have you built walls that God never asked for? Have you drawn lines in your ministry, marriage, or finances that God is asking you to erase? Are you limiting your capacity to grow because you are afraid of what you cannot control? The end of the measuring line begins with a decision: to believe that what God has planned for you cannot be contained in what you have already seen.

Sometimes, God does not give us details because He does not want us to build walls around undeveloped vision. Details are wonderful, but they are not prerequisites for obedience. The Israelites had no GPS in the wilderness. The cloud and the fire were their only guides. Borderless people move when God moves, even when they do not understand the full picture.

Throwing away the measuring line also means releasing the need to compare. Comparison is another form of spiritual measurement. We measure ourselves against others—how far they have gone, how much they have achieved, how quickly they have grown. But the borderless Kingdom is not a race; it is a calling. Your journey will not look like anyone else's. And that is the point. Borderless people do not compete, they collaborate. They do not envy, they enlarge. They celebrate when others succeed because they know there is no shortage of territory in a Kingdom with no walls.

As we move deeper into this book, we will explore the many dimensions of living in the borderless Kingdom: worship without limits, identity without labels, expansion without apology. But everything starts here, with the decision to drop the measuring line. It is a personal revolution. It is the moment you trade safety for surrender, clarity for calling, and fear for fire.

In the end, what will define your life: what you measured, or what you multiplied?

Will your story be one of safe calculations, or of radical obedience?

Will you leave this world full of untapped potential, or empty from pouring it all out?

The man with the measuring line had good intentions. But good intentions are no match for divine interruptions. Do not be surprised if God disrupts your plans, reroutes your dreams, or tears up your blueprints. He is not being cruel. He is being kind. Because He knows that what He has for you is bigger than what you are trying to measure.

Let this be the end of your measuring line. Let this be the beginning of your borderless journey.

Chapter 2

The Weakness of Man-Made Walls

Walls have always been humanity's answer to fear. From the ancient cities of Mesopotamia to the fortified castles of Europe, from border fences between nations to the unspoken boundaries between social classes, walls have been the default solution for insecurity. They protect, they isolate, they define.

But when God declares in *Zechariah 2* that He will build a city without walls, He is confronting more than architectural design. He is exposing a myth: the belief that man-made walls can preserve what only divine presence can protect.

This is a direct challenge to the way we have structured our lives, our faith, and even our churches. Because walls are not only made of stone and steel. Many of the most dangerous walls are invisible: walls of doctrine, denomination, prejudice, fear, and tradition. They are not seen with the eyes, but they are deeply felt. They divide the body of Christ. They stifle revival. They insulate the heart. And worst of all, they subtly suggest that God must work within human limitations.

Walls are comfortable. They provide a false sense of control. We tell ourselves that as long as we are inside the walls, we are safe. But what we often fail to realize is that these same walls also keep us trapped. They restrict movement, they confine vision, they discourage risk, and they tell God, *"You can move, but only within these limits."*

The myth of man-made walls is the belief that we can construct something strong enough to protect God's purposes without compromising His presence. But God never called us to build boundaries around His glory. His presence was always meant to overflow. From Eden's Garden to the tabernacle, from the temple to Pentecost, the story of Scripture is the story of God moving beyond borders. He is not a God who dwells in carefully curated spaces. He is a consuming fire, a rushing wind, a breaking wave, and He has no intention of being boxed in.

Walls Built by Religion

Perhaps the most deceptive of all walls are those built by religion. They appear righteous. They are often well-intentioned. Yet they are just as dangerous. Religious walls are built when rules replace relationship, when tradition takes precedence over truth, and when the comfort of routine outweighs the risk of obedience.

Jesus faced these walls constantly. The Pharisees were experts at building religious barriers. They created systems to regulate holiness: rules about washing hands, observing the Sabbath, and determining who could eat with whom. These structures were meant to preserve God's law, but over time they became substitutes for intimacy with God Himself. The law became a lid, the synagogue became a cage, and the people, rather than being led into freedom, were trapped behind doctrines they did not understand and could not escape.

Jesus broke every one of those walls. He touched lepers. He healed on the Sabbath. He spoke to Samaritan women. He forgave prostitutes. He welcomed children. He dined with sinners. In doing so, He revealed the heart of the Father—a heart not confined by ceremonial purity or social expectation.

The Church today must ask itself: What religious walls have we built?

Have we created boundaries that keep certain people out?

Have we elevated our style of worship, our form of dress, or our theological systems to the point where they exclude those who do not look or sound like us?

Have we turned our pulpits into fortresses, our altars into stages, our denominations into tribes?

If so, we have fallen for the myth. We have believed that God needs our fences. But He doesn't. What He needs is our surrender. The borderless Kingdom cannot be contained in Sunday services, church programs, or leadership structures. It spills over, it breaks in, it shows up in prisons, in nightclubs, in villages, and in boardrooms. The moment we try to confine it, we betray it.

Walls Built by Culture

Another kind of wall is built not by religion but by culture. These are the barriers that separate races, classes, and nations. They are often reinforced by history and power. Cultural walls tell us who belongs and who does not. They tell us which language is superior, which skin color is desirable, which customs are acceptable. These walls are not always shouted; they are whispered. They live in our hiring practices, our church leadership teams, our marriage expectations, and our social circles.

The early church faced these walls head-on. In *Acts 10*, Peter is confronted with a vision that turns his entire worldview upside down. God tells him to eat animals that the law once declared unclean. Peter resists, citing tradition. But God responds, *"Do not call anything impure that God has made clean."* The vision was not just about food; it was about people. Moments later, Peter is invited into the home of Cornelius, a Gentile, where the Holy Spirit falls in power, no Jewish ceremony required.

It was a clear message: *The walls are coming down.*

The Gospel is not Jewish. It is not Roman. It is not Western. It is not American. It is not Black or White or Brown. The Gospel is global, multicultural, multilingual, and transgenerational. It is not confined by geography or ethnicity. Any church that builds cultural walls around the Gospel has stopped preaching the true Gospel.

Revival does not favor culture, it transcends it. When the Holy Spirit fell in *Acts 2*, people from every nation heard the message in their own language. That was not merely a miracle of speech, it was a prophetic declaration. The Kingdom of God is not a monoculture. It is a symphony. And in that symphony, every tribe and tongue matters.

To live in the borderless Kingdom is to confront our cultural biases. It is to tear down the walls we were raised with. It is to see the image of God in people who do not vote like us, look like us, or worship like us. It is to resist nationalism and embrace Kingdom citizenship. Because in the end, every earthly culture is temporary. Only the culture of heaven is eternal.

Walls Built by Offense

Another wall we must confront is the wall of offense. This is a deeply personal wall, yet one of the most common. When we are hurt, misunderstood, betrayed, or overlooked, our natural response is to build walls around our hearts. These walls are meant to keep pain out, but they also keep healing out.

Offense is a silent killer. It creeps in subtly: through a word not spoken, a gesture misread, a promotion denied, a wound reopened. Over time, offense hardens into bitterness. And bitterness, if left unchecked, becomes a fortress. People who live behind the wall of offense cannot receive love freely, cannot trust others deeply, and cannot grow spiritually.

Jesus warned that in the last days, *"many will be offended, and will betray one another, and will hate one another."* The devil knows that offended people are paralyzed people. They stop moving forward, they stop taking risks, they stop being vulnerable, and they eventually stop hearing from God.

The borderless Kingdom cannot thrive where offense is nurtured. Forgiveness is the wrecking ball that tears down emotional walls. It is not a feeling; it is a choice. A decision to release those who hurt us and reclaim our freedom.

When Jesus hung on the cross, betrayed by friends and tortured by enemies, He tore down the wall of offense with one prayer: *"Father, forgive them."* If He could say that with nails in His hands, surely, we can say it with wounds in our hearts.

Forgiveness does not mean what happened was acceptable. It means you are no longer willing to let it define your boundaries. You are choosing to live borderless, not bitter.

Walls Built by Fear

Fear is perhaps the most powerful wall-builder of all. It whispers lies about the future. It paralyzes dreams. It exaggerates risks and minimizes promises.

Fear says; *"Stay inside. Don't try. Don't trust. Don't believe."*

The children of Israel knew this wall well. When they reached the edge of the Promised Land, they sent spies to assess the territory. Ten of them came back with a fearful report: *"We are like grasshoppers in their eyes."* That one statement built a mental wall that kept an entire generation out of their destiny. Not because God was unable, but because fear was louder than faith.

The myth of man-made walls thrives in environments of fear. We build doctrines around what we fear. We create church cultures that avoid anything messy, risky, or unexplainable. We spiritualize caution. Yet Jesus did not come to keep us safe. He came to make us dangerous. Dangerous to darkness, dangerous to despair, dangerous to the myth that says God can only move within predictable boundaries.

Paul told Timothy, *"God has not given us a spirit of fear."* Yet many believers live as if fear were their spiritual gift. They avoid people they are called to love. They delay assignments they are called to fulfill. They water down messages they are called to preach. All because the wall of fear feels more secure than the freedom of obedience.

But the Kingdom is not built by fear, it is built by fire. And fire cannot be contained behind walls. It spreads, it leaps, it consumes. That is why God did not say He would give Jerusalem iron gates or stone towers. He said He would be *"a wall of fire around her."* Not a wall of fear, but a wall of fire.

When you choose faith over fear, you demolish the myth. You live borderlessly, you speak boldly, you move prophetically, and you become a walking contradiction to the spirit of this age.

Tearing Down the Walls

So, what must we do? We must first acknowledge the walls we have built, around our churches, our families, our dreams, and our hearts. Then we must partner with the Holy Spirit to tear them down. It will not be easy. Walls provide safety, but they also produce stagnation. And the Spirit of God never rests in stagnant places.

The borderless Kingdom is not just a theological idea. It is a lifestyle of surrender. It is a refusal to let religion, culture, offense, or fear define what God can do in and through us. It is a call to live unguarded, unmeasured, and unafraid. It is the posture of revival, the atmosphere of awakening, the heartbeat of heaven.

Let this be your declaration: *No more walls.*

Not in my thinking.

Not in my relationships.

Not in my worship.

Not in my obedience.

God is building something without boundaries. And you are part of it.

The Power of Faith in a Wall-less World

"For I, declares the Lord, will be a wall of fire around her, and I will be the glory in her midst."— **Zechariah 2:5**

Chapter 3

The Power of Faith in a Wall-less World

When God announced through Zechariah that Jerusalem would be a city without walls, He was not simply describing a new urban layout; He was redefining how His people were to live, believe, and move. A wall-less city meant exposure. It meant risk. It meant being dependent not on bricks and boundaries, but on the invisible yet invincible protection of God Himself.

To dwell in such a reality required more than tradition, more than doctrine, and more than good intentions. It demanded faith; deep, raw, uncompromising faith. The kind of faith that thrives not in the safety of the known, but in the wildness of God's promises.

In the natural world, walls provide a sense of stability. They enclose and protect. They create perimeters that tell us what is safe, what is ours, and what lies beyond. But in the spiritual realm, the absence of walls is not a threat; it is an invitation. An invitation to live by a different kind of blueprint, one not drawn by architects but by the Spirit.

In a wall-less world, *faith becomes your compass, your anchor, and your fortress*. Without faith, such a world feels dangerous. With faith, it becomes destiny.

Faith Is the Language of the Borderless

The borderless Kingdom is governed by a different set of rules than the kingdoms of this world. While earthly systems rely on proof, precedent, and prediction, the Kingdom of God is advanced by belief, vision, and obedience.

Hebrews 11 introduces us to the great hall of faith, a list of men and women who achieved the impossible by trusting in the invisible. Their stories are not tales of cautious wisdom, but of wild faith.

Noah built an ark before the rain came. Abraham left his homeland before he knew the destination. Sarah believed for a child long after her womb had dried up. Moses walked into Pharaoh's courts with nothing but a stick.

These were not strategists, they were believers. They pioneered a wall-less world, moving at the word of God when nothing else made sense.

Faith is not a supplement to the Christian life; it is the essence of it. *Without faith, it is impossible to please God.* Why? Because God is borderless, and only faith can engage a God who lives beyond limits.

Faith is not just how we start the journey; it is how we survive the wilderness, cross the Jordan, and take the land. It is how we live when the walls are down and the winds of uncertainty are blowing.

Faith Transcends Logic

One of the greatest obstacles to faith in a wall-less world is our addiction to logic. Logic is a gift, but it is not Lord. Logic tells us to stay within what is safe and measurable. It tells us not to walk on water because gravity wins. It tells us not to give what we cannot afford, not to dream what we cannot fund, and not to believe what we cannot prove.

But the borderless Kingdom calls us into a different kind of thinking.

When Peter saw Jesus walking on water, he didn't wait for a scientific explanation. He simply said, *"Lord, if it's You, bid me come."* That was faith. He stepped out of the boat, his only point of security, onto waves that had no structural support. He walked, not because the water became solid, but because the word of Jesus carried him.

Every great move of God in Scripture required someone to bypass logic. Logic would have told David not to fight Goliath. Logic would have told Joshua that marching around a wall would do nothing. Logic would have told Esther that entering the king's chamber uninvited was suicide.

But faith listens to a higher frequency. It obeys the voice that speaks beyond reason.

To live in the borderless Kingdom, we must give up the need for full understanding. God does not owe us an explanation; He offers us an invitation. *Faith is the ability to say yes before you know how.*

Faith Breaks the Fear of Exposure

Walls are built to keep threats out, but they also keep faith in. One of the greatest fears we face is the fear of being exposed, of being vulnerable, unprotected, and out of control.

The children of Israel faced this tension at the edge of the Red Sea. Behind them was Pharaoh's army. Before them was water. They had no weapons, no boats, no backup plan. And in that moment, God said, *"Move forward."*

That instruction made no sense; there was nowhere to go. But when Moses lifted his staff, the waters parted. The sea didn't split before the step; it split because of it.

Faith leads you into places where God has to show up. It refuses to be trapped by past experiences or limited by present obstacles. It says, *"I don't need to know what's next; I just need to know who's with me."*

Exposure becomes power when God is your covering. Without walls, your faith becomes your security. The fire of His presence becomes your shield. And you learn that being vulnerable in obedience is safer than being secure in disobedience.

Faith Releases God's Creative Power

Faith is not merely reactive, it is creative. Faith does not just respond to God's word; it partners with God to create new realities.

Jesus said, *"If you have faith as small as a mustard seed, you can say to this mountain, 'Move,' and it will move."* Faith speaks. Faith creates. Faith moves things.

In a borderless Kingdom, this creative capacity is crucial. You will often be sent to places that have no structure, no resources, and no path. Faith does not wait for provision to appear; it calls it forth.

When Elijah was fed by ravens and drank from a brook, he was not living in ideal conditions. He was operating in faith. When the widow gave her last meal to the prophet, she was not being reckless, she was partnering with creative provision. The jar of oil and the bin of flour did not run out. Why? Because faith stepped in where logic ended.

Faith Cultivates Forward Movement

Walls, whether physical, emotional, or spiritual, create stagnation. They make us settle. They make us complacent. But faith always moves. It is inherently forward.

Abraham was *"looking for a city whose builder and maker is God."* He never stopped moving. Paul declared, *"I press on toward the goal."* He was always advancing.

In a wall-less world, faith is your movement. It compels you to take territory, not just spiritually but practically. It moves you to start the business even if the capital is low. It moves you to write the book even if you don't have the publisher. It moves you to plant the church, launch the ministry, forgive the offender, or travel to the mission field, not because the path is clear, but because the promise is sure.

Faith does not consult your bank account, your education, or your connections. It listens for the voice of God and moves in response. That is how the borderless Kingdom expands, not by cautious planners, but by courageous believers.

Faith Honors God's Timing

In a world addicted to speed and instant results, faith calls us to a different rhythm. It teaches us to trust God's timing, even when it contradicts our own.

Joseph had a dream but waited over a decade to see it fulfilled. David was anointed king as a teenager but didn't sit on the throne for years. Jesus waited thirty years to begin a three-year ministry. Why? Because faith trusts the pace of purpose.

In a borderless Kingdom, timing is not dictated by deadlines but by discernment. Faith says, *"I'll wait when God says wait, and I'll move when He says move."*

The wall-less life is one of patience, perseverance, and prophetic obedience. Faith allows you to rest in the in-between, knowing that delays are not denials, they are developments.

Faith Defeats the Fear of Failure

Perhaps one of the most paralyzing fears in a wall-less world is the fear of failure. Without walls to hide behind, every act of faith feels like a risk.

What if I step out and fall? What if I believe and nothing happens? What if I give and go broke?

Faith silences these questions with one truth: *obedience is never failure.*

Success in the Kingdom is not measured by outcome—it is measured by obedience. Peter may have sunk, but he walked farther than the eleven who stayed in the boat. Abraham may have wandered, but he became the father of nations. Paul may have been imprisoned, but he wrote the letters that shape Christianity.

The borderless Kingdom assumes risk. It is not a safe space; it is a sacred space. And in that space, you will make mistakes. You will misstep. You will face resistance. But if you walk in faith, you will not walk alone.

A Faith That Fills the Empty Places

Faith is the lifeblood of the wall-less life. It fills the gaps where walls once stood. It lights the path where borders once blocked. It becomes your currency in the Kingdom, your access to miracles, and your confidence in uncertainty.

To live in the borderless Kingdom is to live in a constant state of surrender and expectation.

It is to say, *"Lord, I don't need a wall—I need Your word. I don't need a plan—I need Your presence. I don't need security—I need Your Spirit."*

Faith is not a leap into the dark; it is a step into the light you cannot yet see. It is trusting that if God has called you beyond the walls, He has already gone ahead of you. It is believing that what lies beyond the edge of safety is not chaos, but glory.

So let the walls fall. Let the fears break. Let the logic rest. And let faith rise. Because in a wall-less world, *faith is the foundation of everything.*

Chapter 4

A City Without Fear

Imagine a city without walls in ancient times: a city wide open to marauders, wild animals, enemy armies, and thieves. To the natural mind, such a city is not brave, it is foolish. A city without walls appears vulnerable, fragile, and dangerously exposed.

And yet, in *Zechariah 2*, God declares this very vision:

"Jerusalem will be a city without walls because of the great number of people and animals in it. And I myself will be a wall of fire around her," declares the Lord, "and I will be the glory within her."

This was not simply a logistical update about urban planning; it was a divine declaration about the nature of His Kingdom.

God was not just tearing down walls. He was tearing down fear.

Fear Is the Real Enemy

The absence of physical walls is not the true threat; fear is. Fear paralyzes purpose, drains hope, and distorts reality. It is fear—not lack of resources, not enemies, not failure, that most often keeps people from walking in their full destiny.

The Israelites wandered in the wilderness for forty years, not because Egypt was too strong, but because fear of the unknown overtook faith in the promise.

When God said Jerusalem would have no walls, He was offering something better than stone: His presence. Yet that offer can only be fully embraced by those who reject fear.

Fear whispers lies in the voice of reason. It cloaks itself in caution, wisdom, and practicality. Sometimes it sounds like quiet resignation: *"I'm not ready." "This will never work." "What if I fail?"*

But every time fear becomes the guiding voice, the Kingdom shrinks. Walls go up. Territory is lost.

A city without fear isn't fearless because there are no threats; it is fearless because it has the right perspective of God's presence. Fear doesn't disappear because danger is gone, it disappears because faith in God's nearness grows louder than the threats.

The Architecture of Divine Confidence

When God declares, *"I will be a wall of fire around her,"* He is not abandoning protection, He is upgrading it.

Fire is dynamic. Unlike stone, fire moves, breathes, and consumes. Fire symbolizes divine presence, holiness, and supernatural protection. Throughout Scripture, fire appears when God is making Himself known or defending His people: the burning bush, the fire on Mount Sinai, the pillar of fire that led Israel through the wilderness.

Why fire? Because fire cannot be scaled, chiseled, or breached. Enemies can climb over brick, but no one dares walk through the consuming fire of God.

This kind of protection does not invite complacency, it demands intimacy. In a wall-less city, your security depends not on your ability to build but on your ability to abide.

Divine confidence isn't arrogance, it is dependence. It is the calm assurance that *"God is with me; therefore, I will not fear."*

As Psalm 27:1 declares: *"The Lord is my light and my salvation; whom shall I fear?"*

Fear Versus Glory: Two Incompatible Atmospheres

Fear and glory cannot coexist. One will always displace the other. That is why, in Zechariah's vision, God promises not only to be a wall of fire around Jerusalem but also to be *"the glory within her."*

Fear resides where glory is absent. But where the manifest presence of God is dwelling richly, fear has no oxygen. It dies in the atmosphere of glory.

Glory transforms timid believers into bold witnesses. In *Acts 4*, after praying together, the early believers were *"filled with the Holy Spirit and spoke the word of God with boldness."* Glory released courage. The fire of His presence burned away their fear.

Glory is not ambiance, it is power. It turns hidden gifts into blazing ministries. It transforms closed hearts into open doors.

The Fear of Vulnerability

Many fear a wall-less world not because they hate freedom but because they hate exposure.

Walls provide emotional security. They give the illusion of control. But vulnerability is the birthplace of miracles.

- *Peter could not walk on water until he stepped out.*
- *The bleeding woman could not be healed until she reached forward.*
- *Bartimaeus could not receive sight until he cried out above the crowd.*

Vulnerability is the admission that we need God, and that is where His power meets us.

A city without fear embraces vulnerability as strength, not weakness. The fire of God doesn't destroy vulnerability, it sanctifies it.

The Cycle of Fear and Control

Fear creates a cycle of control. We fear loss, so we control people. We fear failure, so we micromanage results. We fear rejection, so we edit ourselves to be accepted.

But control is just a substitute for trust. And in the borderless Kingdom, *trust is non-negotiable.*

When Jesus said, *"Do not worry about tomorrow,"* He was not offering a cliché, He was giving a command. Worry is not the fruit of the Spirit; it is the product of fear sitting where faith belongs.

Cities built on control are doomed to stagnation. Cities built on trust become centers of revival.

Warfare in a Fear-Free Zone

A city without fear is not a city without enemies, it is a city with superior vision.

Living without fear doesn't mean you won't hear the threats. It means you won't bow to them.

The Apostle Paul faced shipwrecks, imprisonment, and betrayal, yet he declared: *"None of these things move me."* His security was not in earthly safety but in eternal purpose.

The enemy thrives in atmospheres of fear. But when fear is absent, he loses leverage. He can attack, but he cannot conquer a fearless Church.

Raising a Fearless Generation

In today's world, anxiety has become an epidemic. Fear wears many disguises such as *depression, hesitation, social withdrawal, indecision, and even rage.* Yet the borderless Kingdom is birthing a generation that is learning to live from a different narrative. Young believers are arising with a hunger for authenticity and a rejection of superficial faith. They do not want religion; *they want reality.* They are willing to go without walls if it means they will encounter the glory of God.

To raise a fearless generation, we must teach them not simply how to survive but how to *host the presence of God*. We must train them not only in doctrine but also in discernment. They must understand that courage is not the absence of fear; it is the decision to move forward in spite of it.

Fearless faith is forged in the fires of worship, prayer, and the Word. It is not the product of hype but of *habitation*. If we desire our children to live in a world without walls, they must first learn to live with a heart free from fear.

Practical Steps to Displace Fear

1. **Immerse Yourself in Truth**: Fear thrives on lies. God's Word is the sword that cuts through deception. Memorize scriptures that remind you of *His nearness* and *His power*.

2. **Practice Vulnerability**: Be honest with God and others about your fears. Hiding fear gives it power. Naming it exposes its weakness.

3. **Worship Relentlessly**: Fear cannot coexist with worship. Praise shifts the atmosphere, silences anxiety, and invites glory.

4. **Pray Boldly**: Do not limit yourself to safe prayers. Pray for miracles, pray for nations, and pray for open doors. Bold prayer builds fearless faith.

5. **Take Faith-Filled Risks**: Begin with small steps. Speak up in the meeting, apply for the job, share your story. Faith grows through practice and expression.

6. **Surround Yourself with Fire Carriers**: Community is essential. Stay connected to those who remind you of your identity and of what God has spoken.

Final Declaration: Fear Has No Home Here

The borderless Kingdom is not a utopia without challenges. It is a divine realm ruled by the presence of God, where fear is not needed, not tolerated, and not empowered. In this Kingdom, the walls are down but the fire is up. And wherever the fire burns, fear must flee.

You are called to live in a city without fear, not because threats disappear, but because your trust is anchored in the One who never fails. Let your life become a testimony of *fearless obedience, unshakable confidence,* and *unquenchable fire.*

The wall is gone. The fire surrounds you. The glory fills you. *Fear has no home here.*

Chapter 5
The Glory Within Her

"And I will be the glory in her midst."
—Zechariah 2:5

When God declared that Jerusalem would be a city without walls, He added something radical and profoundly intimate: *"I will be the glory within her."*

It is one thing for God to surround His people, but another for Him to live inside them. This was not a promise of temporary visitation; it was a declaration of permanent habitation. A city without walls might look exposed, yet it is not vulnerable when it carries the weight of God's presence at its very core. What protects her is not what surrounds her, but what fills her.

To understand what it means to live in a borderless Kingdom, we must grasp the meaning and manifestation of glory. This is not an abstract idea or poetic phrase. In biblical terms, *glory* is weighty. The Hebrew word *kabod* means weight, heaviness, honor, splendor, or abundance. God's glory is the tangible expression of His presence, power, and personality. It is the visible evidence of the invisible God. It is what settled in the Holy of Holies, what filled Solomon's temple, and what shone from Moses' face. And now, it is what God promises will dwell within His city, and by extension, within His people.

This is the beating heart of the borderless Kingdom: we are not only defended by God's fire; we are filled with God's glory.

From Visitation to Habitation

In the Old Testament, the glory of God was largely external. It descended, came upon, and surrounded. The Israelites saw the glory as a cloud by day and fire by night. They witnessed it on Mount Sinai as it wrapped the summit in smoke and thunder.

When Moses finished building the tabernacle, the glory filled it so completely that even the priests could not stand to minister. In Solomon's temple, the same thing happened, the glory of the Lord filled the house so powerfully that it overwhelmed every earthly activity.

But these were moments, glorious, yes, but temporary. The people witnessed God's glory as an event, not a lifestyle. It was something they approached, something they visited, something they prepared for.

In Zechariah's vision, something shifts. God does not say, *"I will come to visit with glory."* He says, *"I will be the glory in her midst."* The word *in* is key. No longer would glory descend and lift; it would dwell. It would become internal, not just external. The glory would not merely come near; it would take up residence.

This shift is foundational to the life of a believer in the borderless Kingdom. We do not live from occasional encounters, but from continual indwelling. The Spirit of God no longer resides in tabernacles made with hands, but in human hearts. We are now temples of the Holy Spirit. The glory that once terrified nations now lives inside those who trust in Christ. And because the glory is within, the believer becomes unshakable, even in a world without visible protection.

The Power of Internal Glory

Why is this significant? Because what is within you determines what comes out of you. If fear, shame, guilt, and insecurity dwell within, they will shape your thoughts, speech, and decisions. But if glory fills you, if the very presence of God lives inside, you will operate from a different dimension. You will carry confidence without arrogance, boldness without pride, humility without weakness, and purity without pretense.

This internal glory empowers you in ways walls never could. Walls restrict, but glory releases. Walls shelter, but glory transforms. With the glory inside, you are no longer reacting to the world, you are influencing it. Your environment no longer defines your atmosphere; you bring the Kingdom with you wherever you go.

The early church understood this. When Peter and John stood before the Sanhedrin, accused and threatened, they did not cower. Scripture says the rulers took note that these men had *"been with Jesus."* That is the effect of internal glory. You do not need a platform to be powerful, nor armor to be dangerous. When the glory lives within, the authority you carry speaks louder than your position.

Living from the Inside Out

Most people live from the outside in. They are governed by circumstances, opinions, and external affirmations. Their joy rises and falls based on outcomes. Their peace is dictated by headlines. Their identity is shaped by success or failure.

But when the glory of God dwells within, everything reverses. You begin to live from the inside out.

Your joy is no longer circumstantial, it is supernatural. Your peace is not passive, it is powerful. Your hope is not naïve, it is anchored. The glory within you becomes the source of wisdom, direction, and discernment.

When others panic, you pray. When others flee, you stand. When others waver, you declare. Because the God of glory is not just beside you, He is inside you.

This kind of life is rare, but it is available. It requires a renewed mind, a surrendered heart, and a daily walk of intimacy. You cannot carry the glory casually. The glory of God demands reverence, purity, and faith. But it also promises transformation, favor, and supernatural strength.

The Glory as Identity

In the wall-less Kingdom, your identity is not defined by what you do, what you have survived, or what others think of you. Your identity is anchored in glory.

You are not simply a believer—you are a carrier. You are not simply forgiven—you are filled. You are not simply redeemed—you are radiant.

When Moses came down from Mount Sinai after spending time with God, his face was so radiant that he had to cover it with a veil. He did not preach a sermon. He did not issue commands. He simply carried glory, and it was visible.

What if believers today were known not just for their creeds but for their countenance?

What if the Church was known not only for its doctrine, but for its demonstration?

What if your life, without saying a word, carried the fragrance and force of glory?

This is the promise of a borderless Kingdom. We do not carry labels; we carry light. We do not promote ourselves; we reflect Him. Glory becomes our identity, and everything we do flows from that awareness.

The Price and Purity of Glory

But glory is not cheap. It cannot be manipulated, faked, or borrowed. It comes through yieldedness, brokenness, and holy hunger.

In *1 Samuel*, when the Ark of the Covenant, the visible sign of God's glory, was captured by the Philistines, a baby was born and named *Ichabod*, meaning *"the glory has departed."* This was a devastating statement. A people without glory are a people without power.

Yet in Christ, we have been restored. The veil is torn. The Spirit has come. The glory is back and this time, it lives in us. But we must steward it with care. We must cultivate purity, not perfection, but posture. God does not look for the flawless; He looks for the surrendered.

When we allow compromise, bitterness, pride, or carnality to govern us, we dim the light. The glory does not leave, but it becomes obscured. Just as clouds dim the brightness of the sun, sin clouds the expression of glory. But the moment we repent, the glory shines again. Restoration is instant when humility is sincere.

In a wall-less Kingdom, holiness is not legalism, it is protection. The fire of God surrounds us, but the glory of God transforms us. Holiness keeps the channel clear and ensures that what God has deposited flows freely.

Glory and Mission

The glory within is not for private enjoyment; it is for public engagement. It is not a trophy; it is a tool. Glory empowers mission. It emboldens the Church to heal the sick, raise the dead, confront injustice, and proclaim truth. It is not a warm feeling in worship; it is the power to live and lead in hostile spaces.

Jesus, the embodiment of glory, moved among lepers, sinners, and Pharisees alike. He wept at tombs, overturned tables, and washed feet. His glory was not distant, it was disruptive. And we are called to do the same.

When glory fills you, you become a change agent. Not because of charisma, but because of content. The content of your life filled with the Spirit, shaped by the Word, and led by love becomes a conduit for Kingdom transformation.

This is why revival does not begin in pulpits; it begins in people. When enough individuals carry the glory of God into their homes, businesses, schools, and communities, the atmosphere shifts. The borderless Kingdom begins to invade the boundaries of this world.

Hosting the Glory

To live with the glory within is to cultivate a lifestyle of hosting. Just as a good host prepares the environment for a guest, so we prepare our hearts for the continual presence of God.

This does not mean you are always on your knees or disconnected from life. It means you are aware, you are listening, and you are yielded.

Hosting glory requires creating margin. Busyness chokes awareness. Noise silences discernment. If we want to carry the glory with clarity, we must make space. This may mean turning down good things for God things. It may mean quiet mornings, fasting, worship, or simply pausing to listen.

It also means honor. God does not dwell where He is treated casually. When you revere His presence, through obedience, humility, and awe, you become a house of glory. Your life becomes a sanctuary. And the line between sacred and secular disappears, because everything you do becomes worship.

When Glory Rests on a People

Something powerful happens when not just individuals, but communities, carry the glory.

The early church in Acts was not impressive by worldly standards. They had no buildings, no budgets, and no social capital. But they had glory. And with that glory came miracles, multiplication, and unstoppable momentum.

In Acts 5, it says people brought the sick into the streets so that even Peter's shadow might fall on them and heal them. That was not because Peter was famous, it was because the Church was saturated with glory.

Imagine churches where the glory is so strong that addictions break during worship. Imagine cities where violence decreases because the glory rests on neighborhoods. Imagine a generation so radiant with God's glory that compromise becomes unfashionable.

This is not fantasy, it is prophecy. In Haggai, God says, *"The glory of this latter house shall be greater than the former."* In other words, what is coming will exceed what has been. The Church is not in decline; it is in refinement. And out of that fire, a glorious people are emerging.

Living as Carriers of Glory

In the borderless Kingdom, we do not depend on walls, systems, or strategies. We live from the inside out. We are not protected by our plans; His presence protects us. We are not secured by our buildings; we are secured by His glory.

"And I will be the glory within her." This promise is not poetic; it is prophetic. It is your inheritance.

You were made to carry glory, not guilt. You were made to shine, not shrink. You were made to walk into dark places and radiate the light of God, not by effort, but by essence.

The walls are gone. The fire surrounds you. And the glory lives inside you.

Let that truth define your prayers. Let it shape your identity. Let it inform your leadership. Let it guard your heart. Let it fill your home.

You are not waiting for glory; you are walking in it.

Now go. Be the city without walls. Be the dwelling place of glory.

Chapter 6

Borderless Worship

In a Kingdom with no walls, worship cannot be confined. Worship is not the warm-up to a sermon, nor is it a stylistic expression or a denominational hallmark. Worship is the atmosphere of the borderless Kingdom. It is the language of heaven and the posture of the heart that hosts the presence of God.

In Zechariah 2, when God says He will be the glory within His people, that glory does not only demand reverence, it draws worship. And that worship is not regulated by buildings, music genres, or rituals. It is *borderless*.

Worship that pleases God does not need a location; it needs a revelation.

Jesus addressed this in John 4 when He encountered the Samaritan woman at the well. She raised the theological debate of her day: Should worship happen on the mountain of Samaria, or in the temple at Jerusalem? Jesus answered not with a location but with a new framework: *"A time is coming and has now come when the true worshipers will worship the Father in spirit and in truth."* He redefined worship by removing geographical restrictions. He tore down the wall between sacred and secular, between "here" and "there." Jesus announced the arrival of *borderless worship*.

Worship Beyond Buildings

One of the most common ways we have confined worship is by reducing it to a place. For centuries, temples, cathedrals, and church buildings have been viewed as the only legitimate space for meeting with God. While gathering in sacred spaces is valuable, the danger arises when the building becomes a box and the box becomes a prison.

In the borderless Kingdom, worship breaks out of the building and invades every space, your living room, your office, your car, your kitchen, the park, the prison, even the boardroom. God is not more present in a cathedral than He is in a hospital room. He is not more attentive on Sunday morning than He is on a Thursday afternoon. His presence does not reside in stained glass or wooden pews; it resides in hearts that are surrendered.

The early Church understood this. Persecuted and scattered, they met in homes, caves, markets, and deserts. They sang in chains and worshiped in secret. Their worship was not hindered by lack of structure; it was liberated by the absence of restriction. Without formal temples, their hearts became portable altars.

Today, we witness a reformation in worship that mirrors the early Church. Worship is going digital. It is going underground. It is going viral. It is happening in nations where public gatherings are illegal and in nations where worship is unpopular. Yet the fire continues to burn, not because of freedom of religion, but because of the freedom of revelation.

Wherever there is hunger, there is an altar.

Worship Beyond Style

Another border we must tear down is the one built by stylistic preference. For many, worship has been reduced to debates about music: hymns versus choruses, gospel versus contemporary, loud versus quiet, traditional versus modern. These stylistic divides, while seemingly harmless, often reveal deeper divisions, generational, racial, and theological.

In a borderless Kingdom, worship cannot be confined to a genre. God is not moved by chord progressions, playlists, or instruments. What moves His heart is not the song itself, but the spirit in which it is sung.

Psalm 96:1 declares: *"Sing to the Lord a new song; sing to the Lord, all the earth."* This call is not a musical competition but a global invitation. The *new song* is not necessarily a fresh composition, but a fresh expression, worship that arises from a current revelation of who God is and what He is doing.

The phrase *"all the earth"* reminds us that worship is not a Western construct. It is global. It sounds different in

Nigeria than in South Korea. It moves differently in Brazil than in Finland. And that diversity is not a problem to solve, it is a beauty to celebrate.

In heaven, every tribe and tongue worship together. That is the sound we should strive for on earth.

Worship Beyond Denomination

Denominational walls are some of the most stubborn barriers in the body of Christ. We divide ourselves over theology, history, and practice. While theological clarity matters, the unity of the Spirit matters more.

Worship is one of the few places where true unity is possible, even among doctrinal diversity. Presbyterians, Pentecostals, Catholics, Baptists, Methodists, Charismatics, and non-denominational alike can join their voices to exalt the same Savior.

The borderless Kingdom does not ignore doctrine, but it refuses to let doctrine divide where love can unify. Worship can heal what walls have broken. When believers gather not to debate but to adore, heaven draws near. Offense falls. The focus returns to the only One who is worthy.

True worship disarms pride, deconstructs self-righteousness, and unifies the body around the throne.

Worship Beyond Emotion

Emotion often accompanies worship, tears, shouting, dancing, silence, or laughter. All are valid expressions, but worship built only on emotion becomes unstable.

Borderless worship is built on revelation, not just reaction. It is rooted in the knowledge of who God is, not only how we feel in the moment.

This is why Paul and Silas could sing at midnight in a prison, not because their circumstances were pleasant, but because their God was worthy.

In a wall-less world, worship cannot be circumstantial; it must be covenantal. It is Job declaring, *"Though He slay me, yet will I trust Him."* It is Habakkuk saying, *"Though the fig tree does not blossom… yet I will rejoice in the Lord."*

This worship does not wait for goosebumps. It chooses to bow. It chooses to bless. It chooses to sing when the soul is heavy. And that kind of worship invites the supernatural.

Worship as Warfare

Worship is not only adoration, it is warfare. In a Kingdom without borders, worship becomes the strategy for taking ground.

When Joshua led Israel into Jericho, the walls fell not by military might, but by a shout of praise. When Jehoshaphat faced an overwhelming army, he sent singers ahead, and God ambushed the enemy.

Worship shifts atmospheres. It confuses demonic strategies. It breaks chains and opens prison doors. In Acts 16, Paul and Silas prayed and sang at midnight. Suddenly, the prison shook, the doors opened, and every chain fell off.

Why? Because worship invites heaven's intervention.

In the borderless Kingdom, we do not fight with swords, we fight with songs. We do not argue with darkness, we worship until light breaks in. [1]

A worshiping people are a warring people, and wherever worship rises, strongholds fall.

Worship and Presence

The ultimate goal of worship is not breakthrough, it is presence. Breakthrough may come, miracles may follow, but the central focus of worship is God Himself.

David, the man after God's heart, longed for presence above all else.

In Psalm 27:4 he says: *"One thing I ask from the Lord… that I may dwell in the house of the Lord all the days of my life, to gaze on the beauty of the Lord."*

The borderless Kingdom raises up Davids, those who carry authority and affection in equal measure, who build

---

[1] The reference to "Davids" highlights biblical leadership grounded in worship before warfare (cf. 1 Sam. 16:7; Acts 13:22). It contrasts divine presence as the ultimate reward of worship with cultural values of production and performance.

altars before they build armies, who sing before they swing. Presence is the reward of worship. In a world driven by production and performance, the presence of God is our only true north.

Worship and Justice

Worship disconnected from justice is incomplete. God is not only interested in our songs. He is interested in our lives.

In Isaiah 1, God rebukes Israel's festivals and music because their hands were filled with injustice: *"Stop bringing meaningless offerings! I cannot bear your worthless assemblies… Learn to do right; seek justice."*

In the borderless Kingdom, worship leads to transformation. It compels us to defend the marginalized, speak against oppression, and care for the orphan and widow. Worship without action is hypocrisy. Worship without love is noise.

True worship touches heaven and transforms earth. It produces generosity, compassion, and courage. It moves believers from pews to protest, from stages to streets, from comfort to calling.

Borderless worship refuses to separate the sanctuary from the city. It knows that the same hands lifted in adoration must also be extended in service.

The Sound of a Borderless People

Borderless worship is not a new sound—it is an ancient one. It is the song of creation, the anthem around the throne, the cry of the redeemed, the groan of the intercessor, the shout of the overcomer.

It is worship without walls. Worship without limits. Worship that rises from prison cells and palaces, from megachurches and mud huts, from whispered prayers and roaring choirs.

This worship cannot be programmed, polished, or controlled. It is Spirit and truth, fire and fragrance. It is rooted in revelation and released in freedom.

In a world obsessed with boundaries, may the Church raise a sound that breaks through every barrier.

Let worship rise, not only from stages, but from living rooms.

Not only on Sundays, but every day.

Not only from the gifted, but from the hungry.

Not only in tongues, but in tears.

Not only with songs, but with surrender.

Let the nations hear the sound of a borderless people—singing not for applause, but for glory.

Because in the borderless Kingdom, the walls are down, but the worship is rising.

"You are not defined by borders, labels, or past mistakes; you are defined by the image of God within you."

Chapter 7

Borderless Identity

In a Kingdom without walls, identity is not defined by nationality, denomination, skin color, or socioeconomic status. It is not limited to family background, education, or past mistakes. In the borderless Kingdom, identity flows from one source alone: God Himself. We are not merely servants of God; we are His children. We are not just recipients of His grace; we are reflections of His nature. The borderless Kingdom begins with a revelation of who you are, but more importantly, *whose* you are.

At the heart of this revelation is one simple but earth-shattering truth: you are made in the image of God. This is not symbolic poetry or religious encouragement. It is divine fact. It is the core of your spiritual DNA. Once you embrace this reality, every earthly label begins to lose its power.

Genesis 1:26–27 sets the tone for human identity: *"Then God said, 'Let us make man in our image, after our likeness…'*

So, God created man in His own image, in the image of God He created him; male and female He created them."

From the beginning, human beings were created to be mirrors of divine nature. We are not gods, but we are like God. We carry His imprint. We echo His character. We were created not merely to survive on earth, but to represent heaven.

The Imprint of Divinity

The Hebrew word for "image" in Genesis is *tselem*, meaning "a shadow, representation, or figure." It implies reflection, not replication. We are not equal to God; we are made to reflect His essence. We are creative because He is creative. We crave justice because He is just. We long for relationship because He is relational. We seek purpose because He is intentional.

Sin distorted that image but did not destroy it. The fall damaged our alignment with God, yet it did not erase our origin. That is why even in fallen humanity, glimpses of divine likeness remain. The desire to love, to build, to forgive, and to sacrifice, all of it echoes Eden.

When Christ came, He did not simply redeem us from sin; He restored us to identity. He modeled what it means to live as a Son of God. Through Him, we now walk not only as saved souls, but as Kingdom ambassadors, citizens of heaven walking in earthly bodies, revealing the heart of God to a broken world.

The borderless Kingdom is a return to Eden, not to a garden, but to a relationship; not to a place, but to a position. And in this Kingdom, identity is not earned, constructed, or performed. It is received.

You Are Not What They Called You

Throughout life, we pick up labels: broken, unworthy, addict, failure, orphan, poor, unwanted, second-best. But heaven calls us something else entirely: *Beloved. Chosen. Royal priesthood. Holy nation. Temple of the Holy Spirit. Joint heir with Christ.*

To walk in the borderless Kingdom, you must lay down every counterfeit identity that life has tried to attach to your soul. You must discard the names people gave you in seasons of pain, trauma, or ignorance. You must stop identifying yourself by your worst mistake or your deepest insecurity. You are not defined by your dysfunction. You are defined by your design.

Jesus encountered people with broken identities, lepers, prostitutes, tax collectors, Samaritans, sinners. Society had labeled and limited them. But Jesus gave them something else: restoration. He never called them by their sin; He called them by their destiny. He never confirmed their shame; He revealed their significance.

In the borderless Kingdom, you must relearn who you are until the Father's voice is louder than your history.

Like God, Representing God

The most radical truth about our identity is this: we are called to represent God on earth. This is not spiritual arrogance, it is theological reality.

2 Corinthians 5:20 declares, *"We are therefore Christ's ambassadors, as though God were making His appeal through us."* An ambassador speaks with the authority of the one who sent him. He does not invent his own message. He represents the interests of the Kingdom he belongs to.

That means when you walk into a room, the Kingdom walks in. When you speak with truth and love, God is speaking through you. When you lay hands on the sick, heaven is extending its power. You are not acting on your own, you are reflecting the One who lives in you.

This revelation is not reserved for elite Christians. It is not for pastors only, or prophets, or miracle workers. It is for every believer. Whether raising children, managing a business, preaching a sermon, or cleaning a floor, you are made in God's image, and you represent His rule in your space.

Identity Is Not Performance

In religious culture, identity is often tied to behavior. If you pray more, you are more spiritual. If you sin less, you are more holy. But in the Kingdom, identity is not achieved, it is received.

Jesus did not perform to prove who He was. At His baptism, before He ever did a miracle, the Father said, *"This is my beloved Son, in whom I am well pleased."* That declaration came before the feeding of the five thousand, before the cross, before the resurrection. The Father affirmed Jesus' identity before His activity.

So, it is with us. Your identity is not the sum of your accomplishments. It is the overflow of divine adoption.

Destroying the Orphan Spirit

One of the greatest enemies to borderless identity is the orphan spirit. This mindset says, *"I am on my own. I must protect myself. I must earn my place. I do not belong."* Even many believers live like spiritual orphans, saved but insecure, forgiven but never free.

But the borderless Kingdom operates from sonship, not slavery. Romans 8:15 reminds us: *"The Spirit you received does not make you slaves… rather, the Spirit you received brought about your adoption to sonship. And by Him we cry, 'Abba, Father.'"*

The orphan spirit lives in fear, but sons live in confidence. Orphans compete; sons collaborate. Orphans perform; sons rest. Orphans strive to be seen; sons know they are celebrated.

When you embrace your identity as a child of God, you stop chasing affirmation and start carrying authority. You stop hustling for validation and start walking in inheritance.

No Borders, No Comparison

In a wall-less Kingdom, comparison is pointless. There is no spiritual class system. There is no elite anointing. There is no "upper class" of holiness. We are all one in Christ.

Galatians 3:28 declares: *"There is neither Jew nor Gentile, neither slave nor free, nor is there male and female, for you are all one in Christ Jesus."* This does not erase uniqueness, it destroys hierarchy.

Comparison is the enemy of identity. It says, *"You are valuable only if you look like them, talk like them, or succeed like them."* But identity in Christ says, *"You are enough because you are His."*

Living From Your Heavenly Passport

To have a borderless identity means you live from a different passport. Philippians 3:20 declares, *"Our citizenship is in heaven."* That means your primary identity is not American, African, Caribbean, Asian, Latin, or European. It is not rich or poor, black or white, educated or uneducated.

Your identity is heavenly. Your culture is Kingdom. Your accent may be earthly, but your language is faith. Your traditions may vary, but your truth is anchored in Christ.

In the borderless Kingdom, your spiritual passport overrides your natural one. You live by heaven's laws. You carry heaven's priorities. You represent heaven's King.

A Culture of Sonship

To build a borderless Kingdom community, we must cultivate a culture of identity. A culture where sons and daughters are raised, not used. Where gifts are developed, not exploited. Where mistakes are met with mercy, not shame. Where people are called higher, not cast away.

In this culture, identity is the foundation for discipleship. You do not disciple someone into performance, you disciple them into revelation.

Jesus did not just teach identity. He lived it. Every miracle He performed, every demon He cast out, every sermon He preached was rooted in one truth: *"I and the Father are one."* (John 10:30)

The Image Is Back

The fall distorted the image. Sin marred our likeness. Fear erased our confidence. But through Christ, the image is restored.

You are not who the world says you are. You are not your past, your pain, or your performance. You are a child of

God. A carrier of glory. A representative of heaven. A mirror of divine nature.

In this borderless Kingdom, your identity cannot be stolen, shaken, or silenced. It is rooted in eternity, revealed in Christ, and empowered by the Spirit.

So, walk boldly. Live freely. Speak confidently. Love deeply. Because you are like God. And you were born to represent Him.

Scientific Echoes of Divine Identity

As we explore the truth that human beings are made in the image of God and are called to represent Him, it is both fascinating and affirming to note that even science is beginning to glimpse this spiritual reality.

Author and researcher Gregg Braden, in his work *Unleashing the God Code*, presents a compelling intersection of ancient scripture, human DNA, and linguistic systems. He suggests that the very makeup of our DNA contains a code that, when translated using

Hebrew letters and their numeric values, spells [2]the name of God. In essence, Braden proposes that embedded in every human cell is the fingerprint of the Creator.

While Braden approaches this discovery scientifically and metaphysically, the relevance to our borderless identity in Christ is striking. His findings echo what Scripture has proclaimed from the beginning: we are not random beings, but intentional creations, living signatures of the divine.

Whether through theology or biology, the message remains the same: you are like God, and you were designed to represent Him.

In a world searching for proof and meaning, such resonance affirms what faith has always declared: your identity is sacred, encoded, and eternal. You are not

---

1. [2] Gregg Braden, *The God Code: The Secret of Our Past, the Promise of Our Future* (Carlsbad, CA: Hay House, 2004). In this book, Braden introduces the concept that a code embedded in human DNA translates to the name of God using ancient Hebrew numerology, suggesting a direct link between divine identity and human biology.

merely made in God's image metaphorically. His imprint exists in the deepest part of your being, spiritually and perhaps even genetically.

This truth strengthens the call to live without borders. You are not a copy of culture; you are a carrier of divine essence. Science may be catching up to what the Spirit revealed in Genesis 1:27: *You were made like Him.*

Chapter 8

Apostolic Expansion: No Borders, Just Territory

This chapter examines how the apostolic spirit propels Kingdom advancement without limitations, showcasing the mission-oriented and pioneering nature of borderless believers.

The borderless Kingdom is not a static place; it is a dynamic movement. It is not defined by where it ends, but by how far it advances. In Zechariah's vision of Jerusalem without walls, the city is overflowing with people, livestock, and divine glory. It is not shrinking; it is spreading. It is not retreating; it is rising. This expansion is not accidental, it is apostolic.

To understand the force behind the borderless Kingdom, we must first understand the apostolic spirit. The word *apostolic* is rooted in the Greek term *apostolos*, meaning "one who is sent." Apostles in the New Testament were not mere figureheads; they were architects, pioneers, foundation layers, and territory takers. They carried Kingdom DNA and released it in unreached places. The apostolic spirit is the engine of divine expansion.

In a borderless Kingdom, we do not build fences; we enlarge territory. We do not settle for comfort; we contend for conquest. We do not plant flags; we establish foundations. Apostolic expansion is not about conquering people; it is about redeeming spaces. It is the call to carry the presence, culture, and authority of the King into every sphere of life: geography, industry, education, family, media, governance, and beyond.

This chapter is a clarion call to apostolic people, to rise up, stretch out, and refuse to live within the safe zones of religion. It is a summons to break free from spiritual stagnation and embrace your assignment as a Kingdom expander.

The Apostolic Nature of God

God is an apostolic God. He is always sending. He sent prophets, priests, kings, and judges. He sent His Word through angels, dreams, and visions. And ultimately, He sent His Son.

Jesus said, *"As the Father has sent Me, so I send you"* (John 20:21). In that moment, He transferred His apostolic mission to His disciples. He did not just save them; He commissioned them. He did not just bless them; He deployed them.

The Gospel itself is apostolic in nature. It does not stay put. It moves. It crosses oceans, climbs mountains, weaves through jungles, and invades cities. It leaps over cultural boundaries and tears down religious walls. It is not passive; it is progressive. The Gospel refuses to be fenced in.

The apostolic God did not come to build a monument; He came to establish a movement. The Church is not a museum of theology; it is a living, breathing force of expansion. The Kingdom of God is not retreating, it is advancing. And apostolic people are the tip of the spear.

The Spirit of Sending

To be apostolic is to live with a sense of divine mission. It is to live *sent*. Every believer may not be called to be an apostle in office or title, but every believer is called to live apostolically.

The Great Commission is not optional. It is not a suggestion; it is the heartbeat of Heaven: *"Go into all the world and make disciples..."* (Matthew 28:19). This is more than evangelism; it is expansion. Discipling nations means influencing cultures, shifting paradigms, and building people who reflect the values of the Kingdom.

Living apostolically means every step you take is sacred. Every job becomes an assignment. Every conversation becomes a mission field. You are not where you are by accident, you are sent. Your workplace is not just a job; it is a jurisdiction. Your neighborhood is not just where you live; it is where you have been planted.

The apostolic spirit sees beyond convenience and embraces calling. It recognizes that comfort zones are graveyards for destiny. Apostolic people are uncomfortable with inaction. They feel the pull of purpose. They are allergic to apathy.

Stretching the Tent

Isaiah 54:2–3 says, *"Enlarge the place of your tent, stretch your tent curtains wide, do not hold back; lengthen your cords, strengthen your stakes. For you will spread out to the right and to the left..."* This prophetic word is a blueprint for apostolic expansion.

Enlargement requires movement. Stretching implies discomfort. Lengthening cords and strengthening stakes means increased capacity. Expansion is messy, inconvenient, and often misunderstood, but it is the nature of the Kingdom.

God never intended for His people to become territorial, defensive, or confined. He called them to be fruitful, multiply, fill the earth, and subdue it. That is not a small-minded mandate, it is a global call. It is the original apostolic commission.

Today, that mandate is still alive. The Church must think beyond sanctuaries and budgets. We must think in terms of nations, generations, and systems. The apostolic spirit does not just build church services; it builds Kingdom ecosystems.

Breaking Borders in Culture

One of the greatest challenges for apostolic people is the cultural border. Culture says, "Stay in your lane." Culture says, "Keep your faith private." But the Kingdom says, *"Go into all the world."* This includes every system of society: education, politics, entertainment, business, and technology.

Apostolic expansion does not mean everyone becomes a preacher. It means everyone becomes a reformer. The teacher who carries Kingdom wisdom is just as apostolic as the pastor on a pulpit. The entrepreneur who funds Kingdom causes is just as missional as the missionary.

The artist who reveals divine beauty in their work is just as prophetic as the intercessor in the prayer room.

The borderless Kingdom does not separate sacred from secular, it redeems the secular by filling it with sacred purpose. Apostolic people do not ask for permission; they walk in authority. They do not wait for culture to invite them; they invade with excellence, truth, and love.

This is how territories shift, not by domination, but by transformation. Apostolic people carry light into darkness and bring Kingdom solutions where systems are broken.

Apostolic Courage

Expansion requires courage. Apostolic people are often misunderstood, criticized, and opposed. Paul was beaten, imprisoned, and rejected, yet he never stopped moving. Why? Because he was possessed by purpose.

If you are going to expand the Kingdom, you must accept this truth: you will not always be applauded. Some will resist your assignment. Others will question your methods. But your obedience is not dependent on consensus, it is rooted in conviction.

Apostolic expansion requires the courage to leave familiar places. Abraham left his homeland. Moses left Egypt. Jesus left the glory of heaven. Paul left the comfort of Pharisaical privilege. Expansion is costly, but it is worth it.

You will have to leave comfort for calling, favor for fire, and reputation for revelation. But what you gain is far greater: territory for God, souls for eternity, and transformation for generations.

Apostolic Architecture

Apostolic people are not just pioneers, they are builders.

Paul said, *"I laid a foundation as a wise master builder"* (1 Corinthians 3:10).

The apostolic spirit sees the invisible and builds what others cannot imagine.

Apostolic architecture is both spiritual and strategic. It lays foundations of doctrine, discipleship, and Kingdom culture. It builds healthy systems, multiplies leaders, and raises up sons and daughters.

Apostolic leaders are not empire builders; they are legacy builders. They do not just fill rooms, they multiply rooms. They do not just grow crowds, they equip saints. Their goal is not attention, it is activation.

Where others see emptiness, apostolic people see opportunity. Where others maintain, they mobilize. Where others protect, they pioneer. They are builders of movements, not monuments.

The Cost of Territory

To take new ground, you must be willing to give up comfort. The children of Israel wanted the Promised Land, but they feared the giants. You cannot enter Canaan with a wilderness mentality.

Apostolic expansion will stretch your time, finances, relationships, and faith. It will expose insecurities and challenge idols. But it will also produce miracles, unlock capacity, and reveal the faithfulness of God in ways you have never known.

The enemy always opposes expansion. He fears it. He knows that one obedient apostolic voice can displace decades of darkness. He knows that one sent person can flip a region, shake a system, or shift a nation.

Here is the truth: the resistance you face is often confirmation of the territory you are called to take.

Apostolic Movement and Momentum

Apostolic expansion is not about speed; it is about momentum. Momentum comes through consistency and endurance. It comes through planting, watering, and trusting God for increase.

Movements do not begin with multitudes, they begin with a mustard seed, a whisper, a conviction, a *yes*. Apostolic people do not wait for big stages; they move with big faith. They understand that small beginnings often lead to significant breakthroughs.

In Acts, the early Church started in an upper room. It expanded to a city. Then to a region. Then to the nations. There was no social media, no funding campaigns, no government approval. Just fire. Just boldness. Just the apostolic spirit.

To recapture that momentum, we must recapture the mandate. We must go. We must send. We must plant. We must risk. We must move.

Apostolic Inheritance

Apostolic people do not just think about their own generation. They think in terms of legacy. Proverbs 13:22 says, *"A good man leaves an inheritance for his children's children."* Apostolic expansion is multi-generational.

What you build now is not just for today, it is for tomorrow. The prayers you pray, the systems you build, the territory you take, all of it becomes inheritance for those who come after you.

Borderless living is not reckless; it is rooted in the long game. It invests in the future. It builds foundations others can stand on. It breaks curses others were bound by. It opens doors others were locked out of.

Conclusion: Sent People, Shifting Kingdoms

The borderless Kingdom expands not because of hype, but because of apostleship. It advances not because of popularity, but because of purpose. It grows not because of noise, but because of obedience.

You are not just saved, you are sent. You are not just delivered, you are deployed. You are not just redeemed, you are released.

Every step you take is territory gained. Every *yes* you speak is a seed planted. Every act of obedience is a door opened. The apostolic spirit is rising, not just in church buildings, but in cities, industries, and nations.

So, go. Stretch wide. Think big. Move fast. Do not ask for permission. Take the land. In the borderless Kingdom, there are no borders—only territory waiting to be taken.

Chapter 9

The Fire on the Borders

In Zechariah 2:5, God gives a powerful promise to Jerusalem: *"I will be a wall of fire around her, and I will be the glory in her midst."* This declaration is one of Scripture's clearest metaphors of divine protection, identity, and presence. In Zechariah's vision, Jerusalem has no physical walls, yet God Himself surrounds the city, not with stone, but with fire.

This image redefines how we understand spiritual boundaries, divine security, and Kingdom expansion. Unlike rigid walls, fire is dynamic, alive, and unstoppable. Human walls can be breached, climbed, or destroyed, but fire represents a living boundary that cannot be bypassed or subdued. When God says, *"I will be a wall of fire,"* He is not offering comfort in metaphor. He is promising a visible shield of glory that both protects His people and defines their spiritual territory.

This chapter explores what it means to be a people whose borders are secured not by human systems, but by the living presence of God revealed through fire. Fire on the borders speaks of protection, purification, separation, presence, and power.

Walls Removed, Glory Revealed

In Zechariah's vision, the removal of walls is not weakness, it is expansion. Ancient cities-built walls for safety, but those same walls created limits. God was declaring that His people were about to outgrow every boundary. The glory of God would overflow the city, and His presence, not human strength, would provide protection.

The absence of physical walls may create vulnerability in the natural sense, but in the Kingdom, it makes space for divine strength. The borderless Kingdom is not defended by armies, locks, or treaties. It is defended by God Himself. His fire is not just a perimeter; it is a living force of power.

Without walls, the people had to live with heightened awareness of God's presence. They could no longer depend on systems or traditions. Their confidence came from the fire that surrounded them. In the Kingdom, the fire of God is our fortress.

Fire as God's Signature

In the Old Testament, fire consistently marked God's presence:

- *It burned in the bush that caught Moses' attention (Exodus 3:2).*

- *It descended on Mount Sinai in glory (Exodus 19:18).*

- *It consumed Elijah's sacrifice on Mount Carmel (1 Kings 18:38).*

- *It appeared as tongues of fire at Pentecost (Acts 2:3).*

Every time God wanted to mark a place, a people, or a movement, He used fire. Fire is His signature; His unmistakable stamp of authenticity. When He promised to be a wall of fire around Jerusalem, He was not only promising safety. He was declaring identity: *"This place belongs to Me."*

The fire on the borders becomes a visible witness. It tells every power of darkness, *"This is God's territory."*

Fire as Purifier and Refiner

God's fire does more than protect—it purifies. Malachi 3:2–3 describes Him as a refiner's fire, purifying His people like gold and silver. Refinement requires heat and exposure. It burns away impurities and strengthens what remains.

The fire on the borders is not just keeping the enemy out. It is transforming the people within. God is not content with a protected people—He desires a holy people.

The borderless Kingdom is not a refuge for compromise, but a furnace where sons and daughters are forged in purity and strength.

Fire as Movement and Mission

In Exodus, the pillar of fire not only protected Israel but guided them. It moved, and they moved with it. In the same way, the fire on the borders does not make us passive survivors, it propels us into mission.

Spirit-filled believers sense the movement of the flame. They look for where God is burning next, what city, what industry, what person needs the Kingdom. The fire becomes both a shield and a launching pad. It defends while it advances.

The Fire at Pentecost: An Internal Border

At Pentecost, fire shifted from external to internal. It rested on the disciples and filled their hearts. For the first time, God's people themselves became the carriers of fire. The border was no longer around them but within them.

Paul later wrote, *"Do you not know that your body is a temple of the Holy Spirit?"* (1 Corinthians 6:19). This truth changes everything: the fire is no longer confined to geography; it travels wherever you go. You are now the moving border of God's Kingdom.

When Fire Becomes a Witness

The presence of fire always draws attention. Moses turned aside to see the burning bush. Israel gathered at Carmel when fire fell on Elijah's altar. Crowds from every nation gathered at Pentecost when fire fell on the disciples.

Fire testifies. Fire reveals. Fire witnesses.

When God marks your life with His fire, you become a living signpost of His presence. People are drawn not to your personality or performance, but to the warmth and safety of the fire you carry. In a world of fear and confusion, fiery believers shine as lighthouses of hope.

Fire as Warfare

Scripture often portrays God's fire as a weapon of warfare. Psalm 97:3 says, *"Fire goes before him and burns up his foes on every side."* Isaiah 66:15 declares that the Lord comes *"with fire… to bring down his anger with fury."*

The enemy cannot pass through fire. Demons flee before it. Witchcraft withers in its presence. Depression breaks under its heat. Fire is not symbolic; it is spiritual reality.

Every believer surrounded by fire becomes a no-go zone for the enemy. The attacks may come, but the fire declares: *"You cannot win."*

Fueling the Fire

In Leviticus 6:13, God commanded: *"The fire must be kept burning on the altar continuously; it must not go out."* The fire came from heaven, but the priests had to sustain it.

The same is true today. The fire of God is divine in origin but human in stewardship. Worship feeds it. Prayer stirs it. The Word sustains it. Fasting clears away the ashes. Prophecy fans the flame.

If the fire in you feels dim, return to the altar. Surrender again. Present yourself as a living sacrifice (Romans 12:1). God is faithful to reignite what He began.

Life Framed by Fire

The fire on the borders is more than imagery, it is the reality of the Kingdom. Where walls once stood, fire now burns. Where fear once ruled, God's presence reigns. Where compromise once lived, holiness now thrives.

You are not surrounded by limits; you are surrounded by fire. So live ablaze. Speak boldly. Expand without fear.

God has already declared: *"I will be a wall of fire around her, and I will be the glory in her midst."*

And that promise is more than enough.

Chapter 10

The Church Without Borders

The church was never meant to be a building. It was never meant to be a time slot, a denomination, or a cultural club. From its inception, the church was a movement, not a monument. It was designed to be a living body of believers empowered by the Spirit, sent into the world to reflect Christ, and called to function without limitations.

The very moment Jesus declared, *"I will build my church, and the gates of hell shall not prevail against it"* (Matthew 16:18), He introduced a global, borderless initiative. It was never meant to be a confined, localized institution.

A borderless church is not simply a poetic metaphor. It is a radical spiritual reality. It is the unstoppable expansion of God's Kingdom through ordinary people carrying extraordinary presence. This chapter explores what it means for the church to live and thrive without borders: geographically, culturally, doctrinally, and spiritually.

To understand the full weight of a borderless church, we must first unlearn centuries of institutionalism that have reduced the church to four walls, Sunday services, and hierarchical traditions. We must return to the original blueprint: where fire fell on people, not pews; where power flowed through fishermen, not pulpits; where cities were shaken, not just sanctuaries filled.

This is not an attack on the physical gathering of believers. Far from it. It is a prophetic cry to reclaim what the church was always meant to be: the visible manifestation of an invisible Kingdom, everywhere, at all times, through everyone.

The Church: A People, Not a Place

In the New Testament, the Greek word for church, *ekklesia*, means *"called-out ones."* It referred not to a building, but to a gathering of people summoned for a purpose. The early church understood this truth. They met in homes, synagogues, marketplaces, and courtyards. Their meetings were alive with power: people were healed, demons were cast out, the Word was preached, and the Spirit was poured out.

The borderless church is a people-centered movement. It cannot be reduced to a denomination, a zip code, or architecture. Wherever believers gather, in corporate boardrooms, living rooms, street corners, or coffee shops, the church is present.

When the church becomes overly tied to buildings, budgets, and branding, it risks forgetting its true identity.

The church was birthed in the upper room, exploded in the streets of Jerusalem, and was scattered through persecution to the ends of the earth. It grew without centralized headquarters, government protection, or formal seminaries. Why? Because the church is not a human invention. It is a divine organism.

You are the church. Not just on Sunday. Not just when you worship. You are the church when you speak life, when you intercede in silence, when you heal the sick, when you mentor a child, when you serve your neighbor, and when you declare truth in the face of deception. *The borderless church lives through you.*

Breaking the Geographical Borders

The early apostles carried the gospel across oceans, deserts, and continents. Paul's journeys stretched from Jerusalem to Rome. Philip ministered in Samaria and Gaza. Thomas traveled as far as India. The Spirit was always pushing the church outward, beyond ethnic comfort zones, beyond cultural norms, beyond natural boundaries.

Today's church must regain that missional mindset. A borderless church does not wait for people to come in. It goes out. It invades nations, schools, government offices, hospitals, and digital spaces. It is fluid, not static; sent, not sedentary.

In this digital age, the borderless church can reach beyond its physical footprint. Online services, livestreamed messages, digital discipleship, and social media missions are expanding Kingdom influence globally. However, this should not replace physical gatherings. It should amplify them. The key is not where the message is delivered, but who carries it and what it contains.

The church without borders refuses to be localized. Whether in persecuted underground gatherings or open-air crusades, its mandate is the same: *"Go into all the world and preach the gospel to every creature"* (Mark 16:15). It crosses barriers not to colonize, but to redeem.

Beyond Cultural Borders

Culture often builds invisible walls between people groups. These walls are formed around race, language, class, tradition, and even fashion. But the gospel tears them down. In Galatians 3:28, Paul declares, *"There is neither Jew nor Greek, slave nor free, male nor female, for you are all one in Christ Jesus."* This is not just a theological idea. It is a Kingdom mandate.

The borderless church is multicultural, multilingual, multiethnic, and multigenerational. It celebrates diversity while remaining rooted in unity. It refuses tribalism and chooses family. It honors tradition but lives by revelation.

It knows that while styles of worship may vary, the Spirit behind them remains the same.

To build a church without borders, we must intentionally resist cultural superiority. Western Christianity is not the default. Neither are African, Asian, or Latin expressions of faith. Every culture brings something beautiful to the global body. The borderless church recognizes this and integrates it, refusing to exalt one expression over another.

Crossing Doctrinal and Denominational Lines

Over time, the body of Christ has fragmented into denominations, many of which formed in pursuit of doctrinal clarity, but some also through offense, ego, and division. While doctrinal integrity is important, it was never meant to replace relational unity.

Jesus prayed in John 17, *"That they may be one, just as we are one."* Unity was not optional to Jesus; it was the goal. A borderless church seeks collaboration, not competition. It focuses on what unites us in Christ, not what separates us theologically.

The days of isolated ministries, siloed congregations, and guarded pulpits are over. In the borderless Kingdom, apostles work with prophets, pastors link arms with evangelists, and churches share platforms, resources, and people to fulfill a common mission. *We are not owners; we are stewards of the same vineyard.*

Destroying Religious Borders

One of the greatest threats to a borderless church is religion, not faith, but the empty structures and systems that exalt form over power. Paul warned of those who have *"a form of godliness but deny its power"* (2 Timothy 3:5). Religion builds walls where God builds bridges. It honors appearances over substance, and fences over freedom.

Jesus constantly confronted the religious systems of His day because they limited access to the Father. They made people jump through hoops instead of bringing them straight to the cross. The borderless church does not create rituals to impress God; it releases people to encounter Him.

In a borderless church, the goal is not institutional loyalty, it is Kingdom citizenship. People do not belong because they filled out a membership form, they belong because they were *born again* into a family of faith.

The Mobilized Body

A borderless church is a mobilized church. It does not wait for people to become perfect before using them. It equips the saints for the work of ministry (Ephesians 4:12). It sees every believer as a potential leader, not a lifelong spectator. It tears down the platform–audience divide and unleashes an army of Kingdom influencers.

In many churches, the pastor is the performer, and the congregation is the crowd. But in the borderless church, the fivefold ministry exists to *activate the many*. Apostles lay foundations. Prophets bring vision. Evangelists ignite urgency. Pastors nurture health. Teachers root people in truth. But the entire body moves together.

The church without borders is not one big meeting, it is millions of missional moments occurring every day around the world. A hug at a hospital, a word of knowledge in a workplace, a testimony shared over dinner, *all of it is church.*

Revival and Persecution: The Flames of Expansion

Historically, the church has grown the fastest during two seasons: revival and persecution. Both tear down borders, one through the outpouring of the Spirit, the other through the stripping away of comfort. In both, the borderless nature of the church shines.

In revival, the Holy Spirit breaks through religious routines. Denominational lines blur as hunger for God rises. Young and old are transformed. Gifts awaken. Cities shake. The church becomes a wildfire.

In persecution, believers are scattered, but the gospel spreads. The underground church in China, the house churches of Iran, the refugee believers of Syria, these are examples of the church thriving beyond control, beyond infrastructure, beyond boundaries.

Revival and persecution are both reminders that the church cannot be confined. *It is a fire, not a fortress. A family, not a facility. A revolution, not a religion.*

The Church in Every Sphere

The borderless church invades not just nations, but *spheres of influence*. Media, education, government, business, arts, and healthcare, all of these become platforms for Kingdom expansion. We were never meant to hide inside churches. We were meant to *disciple nations* (Matthew 28:19).

That means raising Daniels in politics, Josephs in economics, Esthers in diplomacy, and Lydias in commerce. The borderless church does not run from culture, it transforms it. It sends Kingdom-minded people into boardrooms, classrooms, courtrooms, and newsrooms to bring truth, wisdom, and power.

This is not about dominionism, it is about infiltration with integrity. *We do not take over. We serve. We do not impose. We influence. We do not demand. We demonstrate.*

The world will never be changed from a pulpit alone; it will be transformed when the whole church steps into the whole world with the whole gospel.

The Glory Within

Zechariah 2:5 did not just say God would be a wall of fire. He said, *"I will be the glory in her midst."* The fire on the borders protects, but the glory within empowers. The church without borders is not sustained by clever strategies, good lighting, or marketing plans, it is sustained by the glory of God.

That glory is His manifest presence. It is the weight of who He is revealed among His people. When the church prioritizes His glory, everything else aligns. Healings flow. Wisdom comes. Unity increases. Salvation multiplies.

The borderless church does not boast in its size, branding, or cultural relevance. *It boasts in His presence.* If God is not with us, we are just a motivational club. But when His glory dwells, the church becomes irresistible.

Conclusion: A Church That Cannot Be Contained

The future of the church is not mega, it is mobilized. It is borderless, not boxed. It is glorious, not gimmicky. It is fire-marked, not fear-filled. It is global, not grounded in one place.

You are part of this church. You carry its DNA. You are a walking embassy of Heaven. Your living room can become a revival center. Your hands can release healing. Your prayers can shift nations. You are not limited by title, training, or tradition. *You are part of the church without borders.*

So, dream bigger. Pray louder. Walk farther. Love deeper. Preach boldly. Give generously. And live fully surrendered.

Because the borderless Kingdom needs a borderless church, *and the world is waiting for it to rise.*

Chapter 11

The Sound That Produces Uncommon Results

From the dawn of creation, sound has always been an agent of divine power.

In Genesis 1, God spoke, and the universe leapt into existence. "Let there be…" was not mere poetry; it was the command of a King whose voice carried the vibration of life, form, and force.

This divine precedent set the tone for all history:

- *Sound precedes shaking.*

- *Sound initiates transformation.*

- *Sound is Heaven's delivery system for glory, judgment, and revival.*

In a world saturated with noise, the sound that shakes nations is not about volume, it is about authority. It is not the clang of human rhetoric, but the vibration of Heaven moving through yielded vessels on earth. It is the sound of the borderless Kingdom thundering through prophetic voices, worshipping hearts, and apostolic proclamations.

***

This chapter unpacks the theology, history, and practical outworking of the sound that shakes nations. It explores the ways God uses sound to disrupt systems, revive hearts, unify people, and assert His Kingdom in a divided and disoriented world.

As you read, let your ears be opened to hear not just what is being said, but what Heaven is sending.

***

The Voice That Created the World

Before there were nations to shake, there was a voice that created all things. The Spirit hovered, but nothing moved until the voice spoke.

"Let there be light" initiated an irreversible process of formation. Light exploded into being. Skies were divided. Waters were gathered. Life emerged. *Sound activated creation.*

Hebrews 11:3 affirms this truth: *"By faith we understand that the worlds were framed by the word of God, so that the things which are seen were not made of things which are visible."* The Word of God is not ink on paper; it is a cosmic frequency of divine will. Every mountain, molecule, and man still vibrates with the aftershocks of God's initial command.

This is foundational to understanding the power of sound. What God initiates through speech, He sustains through resonance. Therefore, when we align our voices with His, we are not simply expressing opinions, we are echoing eternity. The sound that shakes nations is not innovation, it is synchronization.

The Sound of Deliverance

Throughout Scripture, God has used sound to trigger deliverance. When Israel cried out under Egyptian bondage, their sound reached Heaven, and God responded with fire, plague, and parting seas. Their groaning was not just a complaint; it was a signal. Deliverance is often triggered by a righteous sound.

Consider Jericho. The city was fortified, its walls thick and high. But God did not instruct Israel to bring siege weapons. He told them to walk, stay silent for six days, and then, on the seventh, to release a shout. When they obeyed, the walls fell, not because of the decibel of their shout, but because of their alignment with God's timing and strategy.

This is a pattern: when God's people release the right sound in obedience, structures collapse. Religious strongholds, political oppression, and personal bondage all yield to the sound of Heaven released on earth through believing hearts and unified voices.

The Earth Responds to Sound

The earth is not passive. It responds to prophetic sound. At Mount Sinai, when God descended with thunder and trumpet blasts, the mountain shook violently (Exodus

19:18–19). At Jesus' death, when He cried out in a loud voice and gave up His spirit, the ground quaked, rocks split, and tombs opened (Matthew 27:50–52).

Sound causes shaking because it breaks the static equilibrium of things as they are. It introduces new energy into the system. Spiritually speaking, sound from Heaven releases recalibration. It demands alignment. It disrupts business as usual.

In Acts 4:31, the early church prayed, and the place where they gathered was shaken. They didn't whisper; they lifted their voices in one accord. Their unified sound created a heavenly disturbance that had a tangible impact. *The sound of their agreement echoed with divine power.*

Worship as a Nation-Shaking Sound

Perhaps the most potent and misunderstood weapon in the church's arsenal is worship. True worship is not just musical; it is governmental. It is the throne room meeting earth. When we worship in spirit and truth, we open portals through which Heaven invades history.

Psalm 22:3 declares that God is enthroned on the praises of His people. When believers worship, they are not entertaining, they are enthroning. And wherever God is enthroned, His rule extends. Worship doesn't just affect moods, it affects geography.

In 2 Chronicles 20, King Jehoshaphat faced an alliance of enemy armies. His strategy was unusual: he appointed singers to go ahead of the army, declaring, *"Give thanks to the Lord, for his love endures forever."* As they sang, confusion fell upon their enemies, and the armies destroyed each other. *Their sound triggered divine ambush.*

This is not unique to ancient Israel. In modern revivals, worship has often been the spark that ignited city-wide transformation. From the Welsh Revival to the Azusa Street outpouring, the sound of yielded hearts in worship has preceded cultural shaking.

The Prophetic Voice

Another component of the nation-shaking sound is the prophetic voice. When prophets speak, they do not merely predict; *they declare*. They release Heaven's perspective into earthly timelines. Elijah called down fire. Jeremiah uprooted and planted with words. Ezekiel prophesied to dry bones, and they became an army.

In Ezekiel 37, God told the prophet to speak to a valley of dry bones. As Ezekiel obeyed, the bones rattled, came together, and flesh formed. Yet life only entered them when he prophesied to the wind. This illustrates that sound precedes spirit. Structure comes first, but *breath follows sound.*

Today's prophetic voices are not just for church platforms; they are for national stages, boardrooms, classrooms, and media networks. They carry sound that shakes ideologies, exposes darkness, and catalyzes reform. The borderless Kingdom does not limit prophecy to Sunday services. It sends it into every domain that shapes nations.

The Church as a Sounding Board

The borderless church is not merely a gathering; it is a sounding board for Heaven. It amplifies what God is saying in every generation. It tunes itself to Heaven's frequency and becomes a conduit for transformation.

When Peter preached on Pentecost, he raised his voice, and 3,000 souls were saved (Acts 2:14–41). That sound did not remain in Jerusalem; it reverberated across the Roman Empire. What began with a flame and a voice became a global revolution. The sound birthed a movement.

The modern church must rediscover this authority. Preaching is not opinion-sharing; *it is sound-releasing*. Prophecy is not flattery; *it is truth-declaring*. Intercession is not murmuring; *it is spiritual artillery*. Our pulpits must become launchpads for sound. Our gatherings must become echo chambers for glory. Our voices must be heard beyond our walls.

Sound and Unity

One of the most powerful sounds is the sound of unity. In Acts 2, the Spirit did not descend until the believers were in "one accord in one place." Unity does not just feel good; *it attracts Heaven*. Psalm 133 likens it to oil on

Aaron's beard and dew on Mount Hermon, concluding, *"There the Lord commands the blessing."*

When the church speaks with one voice, nations listen. When believers lift up a singular cry for justice, healing, revival, and righteousness, the sound becomes irresistible. It pierces through politics, religion, and unbelief. It carries weight.

This is why division is so destructive. The enemy fears our united sound, so he sows offense, tribalism, denominationalism, and distraction. But a borderless Kingdom refuses to echo discord. It aligns around Christ and lifts one voice to Heaven — and the nations tremble.

The Sounds of Injustice and Intercession

Every nation has its own sound: the weeping of the oppressed, the shouting of protesters, the rhetoric of politicians, the silence of the abused. But there is also a sound rising from within the Kingdom — *a sound of intercession that responds to injustice with fire.*

In Exodus, the Hebrew slaves cried out, and God heard their groaning. In Revelation, the prayers of the saints rise like incense before the throne, mingled with fire, then cast down upon the earth in judgment (Revelation 8:3–5). Intercession is not passive; *it is combustible.*

The church must recover the sound of travail, not just polished prayers, but groanings too deep for words (Romans 8:26). These groans are birth pangs for national awakening. They are Heaven's language through human vessels. They do not beg; *they birth*. And they do not go unanswered.

Sound in the Marketplace

The sound that shakes nations is not confined to pulpits. It must also resonate in marketplaces; in economics, science, technology, media, and government. Joseph shook Egypt with his sound of strategy. Daniel shook Babylon with his wisdom. Esther saved a people with her voice of courage.

Believers are called to carry the sound of truth and excellence into the systems that shape society. They speak not just with Bible verses, but with innovation, solutions, and supernatural discernment. Their sound is not always loud, but it is undeniable.

In this age of influence, *your podcast can be a pulpit. Your brand can be a trumpet. Your company can be a megaphone.* Every area of your calling is an altar. Every word you speak can carry the vibration of glory. When the righteous rise with sound, nations bend to listen.

The Coming Sound of Glory

There is yet a greater sound on the horizon. Scripture declares, *"The Lord himself will descend from heaven with a shout, with the voice of the archangel and with the trumpet call of God"* (1 Thessalonians 4:16). The second coming of Christ will be announced not silently, but with a cosmic sound that shakes the heavens and the earth.

That final sound will signal resurrection, judgment, and the full manifestation of the Kingdom. Until then, the church is the echo of that coming sound. Every sermon, song, prayer, and prophecy is a rehearsal for the moment the sky splits open.

The sound that shakes nations today is not separate from the sound that ends history. It is the same sound, building, amplifying, resounding through time until the King returns.

Release the Sound

The world is not waiting for another celebrity. It is not desperate for more trends or empty talk. The world is waiting for a sound; a sound born in Heaven, carried by consecrated vessels, released with authority, and echoed by a people who believe what they say.

You are that vessel. The borderless Kingdom flows through your lungs. Do not silence yourself. Do not wait for perfection. Do not apologize for the volume of your conviction. Let the sound rise.

Prophesy. Worship. Declare. Intercede. Testify. Innovate. Speak. Sing. Shout.

Because when the people of God release the sound of the Kingdom, nations do not just listen, *they shake.*

Chapter 12

The Unlimited Concept of the Googleplex: A Borderless Insight

In seeking to understand the nature of God's Kingdom, a realm without walls, limits, or natural boundaries, it is helpful to use metaphors from contemporary culture. These bridges connect abstract spiritual truths with relatable modern images. One such metaphor is the concept of the *Googolplex*. Though rooted in mathematics, this number transcends computation and offers a powerful image of the vast, boundless, and ever-expanding nature of God's Kingdom on Earth.

A *googol* is the digit 1 followed by 100 zeros. For comparison, the estimated number of atoms in the observable universe is around 10^{80}. A *googolplex*, however, is 10 raised to the power of a googol—$10^{\wedge}(10^{100})$. This number is so large it cannot be written out in full, even if we tried to fill the observable universe with digits. The *googolplex* symbolizes the [3]incalculable, stretching human imagination to its limits. When brought into conversation with the Kingdom of God, it illustrates how small human comprehension is compared to divine infinity.

The Kingdom of God is not constrained by geography, ethnicity, culture, time, or mortality. It is, by nature, borderless. It cannot be mapped like earthly empires, nor reduced to buildings or traditions. It expands through faith, flows through revelation, and advances with divine intention. The *googolplex* reminds us that the mind of God operates far beyond human metrics. As Isaiah 55:8–9 declares: *"For my thoughts are not your thoughts, neither are your ways my ways," declares the Lord. "As the heavens are higher than the earth, so are my ways*

---

[3][1] A googolplex is a mathematical concept introduced by Edward Kasner in 1938 to illustrate extraordinarily large numbers. It is defined as 10 raised to the power of a googol (10^{100}), and its magnitude surpasses the number of atoms in the observable universe, making it a useful metaphor for the boundless and infinite nature of God's Kingdom.

higher than your ways." The *googolplex* becomes a prophetic metaphor for how vast those divine thoughts truly are.

Interestingly, the term *Googleplex* was also adopted by one of the most influential companies of our age—Google Inc.—as the name of its headquarters in Mountain View, California. Google's mission, *"to organize the world's information and make it universally accessible and useful,"* reflects a spirit of borderlessness. The Googleplex as a workplace fosters innovation, inclusivity, and an open exchange of ideas—resisting traditional corporate limits. In this way, it reflects a Kingdom principle: truth should be universally accessible to every tribe, tongue, and nation.

In today's world, marked by national, economic, and ideological borders, the Kingdom offers an alternative framework. It is not governed by scarcity but by abundance, not by fear but by faith, not by confinement but by expansion. And this expansion is not chaotic. Like Google's algorithms that sort data with unseen precision, the Kingdom operates strategically; sending people, messages, and movements exactly where they are needed. Matthew 13:33 compares the Kingdom to yeast that permeates an entire batch of dough; quietly, steadily, and irresistibly filling every space.

The Kingdom is not just vast; it is *immeasurably vast*. In our age of constant metrics; likes, shares, steps, salaries; the impact of faith, obedience, presence, and transformation cannot be measured. When Jesus said in John 18:36, *"My kingdom is not of this world,"* He declared a dimension so far beyond earthly systems that even a *googolplex* is only a faint echo of its scale.

This has practical implications. Borderless living means abandoning earthly ceilings and embracing eternal blueprints. Success is not limited to pulpits, salaries, or land ownership. You may never own property, yet God may grant you spiritual authority over entire regions. Your prayers may shift governments. Your books may reach nations you never visit. Your words may travel farther than your feet. As Psalm 19:4 says: *"Their voice goes out into all the earth, their words to the ends of the world."*

Through the lens of the *googolplex*, we begin to dismantle the lie of smallness. You may feel insignificant in the natural, but spiritually you are a divine algorithm, encoded with purpose, empowered by the Spirit, and sent to shift realities. The *googolplex* illustrates that infinite capacity exists when powered by the right energy. For believers, that energy is the Holy Spirit.

Romans 8:11 reminds us: *"If the Spirit of him who raised Jesus from the dead is living in you, he who raised Christ from the dead will also give life to your mortal bodies."* Divine energy is our power source. Unlike human bandwidth, Heaven's system does not crash, lag, or require upgrades. It is eternal and flawless from the beginning.

Another lesson from the *googolplex* is its irreducibility. It cannot be simplified or casually expressed. Likewise, the destiny God places on your life may be too complex to explain. You may not fully understand it yourself, but its power remains. Some things are too vast to be articulated, they must simply be lived and revealed in time.

This perspective transforms leadership and ministry. Many divine callings cannot be fulfilled in a single season or lifetime. Moses saw the Promised Land only from a distance. David prepared for the temple but never built it. Paul sowed into a global church structure he did not live to witness. Each operated by eternal blueprints larger than themselves. Embracing the *googolplex principle* allows us to plant seeds for harvests that may outlive us, valuing alignment with God's purpose over human applause.

The implications reach discipleship as well. We are not called merely to train churchgoers, but to raise cultural reformers, innovators, and nation-shapers. We must disciple believers to think *googolplex*—to dream without limits and lead without ceilings. Scripture itself testifies to Spirit-inspired innovation: blueprints for arks, tabernacles, cities, and nations. Exodus 31:3–5 describes Bezalel as filled with God's Spirit, skill, and knowledge in all kinds of crafts Innovation is not secular, it is sacred.

If Google can build a trillion-dollar empire from organizing man's information, how much more should the Church, who carries the mysteries of Heaven, operate with divine brilliance? We must ask bigger questions: *How do we disciple nations? How do we raise Kingdom disruptors? How do we release prophetic architects, technologists, and apostolic builders?*

The *googolplex* is not just a number, it is a prophetic symbol, pressing us to envision a Kingdom without walls. It echoes Isaiah 54:2: *"Enlarge the place of your tent, stretch your tent curtains wide, do not hold back."* The choice before every believer is clear: live by natural metrics, or live by Kingdom measure.

***

The unlimited concept of the googolplex is not a lesson in mathematics but a summons to faith. It calls us to look beyond the visible, to live in ways that reflect God's limitless nature. It reminds us that the Kingdom is infinite, irresistible, and unstoppable.

"Now to Him who is able to do exceedingly abundantly above all that we ask or think, according to the power that works in us."
— **Ephesians 3:20**

Chapter 13

The Spirit of Limitlessness

The human soul, made in the image of God, was never designed to live confined. Before sin, shame, and systems entered the picture, mankind walked *unashamed, uninhibited, and unrestricted* in the Garden of Eden. The very first chapter of Genesis reveals God's original design:

"Be fruitful, multiply, fill the earth, and subdue it; have dominion..." (Genesis 1:28, NKJV).

These words are not just a commission; they are a prophetic glimpse into the limitless capacity of the human spirit under divine authority.

To understand the *borderless Kingdom*, we must recognize that God's Spirit never creates within the boundaries of fear, lack, or smallness. Everything about the Spirit of God is *expansive*. From the universe He breathed into existence to the indwelling of His Spirit within every believer, the nature of God is growth, increase, multiplication, and dominion. Wherever the Spirit of the Lord is, there is *liberty*—not confinement (2 Corinthians 3:17).

When the Spirit filled the early Church on the day of Pentecost, He did not create a cloistered community, content to celebrate in a single room. He launched a *global movement* that could not be contained by culture, language, ethnicity, or empire. This movement, empowered by the Holy Spirit, defied social norms, political persecution, and religious resistance. Why? Because *limitlessness was woven into its DNA*. What happened in an upper room ignited a spiritual wildfire that spread to nations.

This same Spirit, the one who hovered over the chaotic waters of creation and raised Jesus from the dead, now lives in every believer. Yet, too many Christians live as though they are hemmed in, tied down, and restricted by the visible world. They pray with caution, dream with limitations, and expect only what they can logically calculate. But the *Spirit of Limitlessness* is calling us higher.

The borderless Kingdom cannot be lived out with a *limited mindset*. It requires the radical renewing of our inner perspective. Paul writes in Ephesians 3:20 that God is able to do *"exceedingly abundantly above all that we ask or think, according to the power that works in us."* That power is not a distant force, it is the Spirit within, pushing us beyond mental boundaries into divine possibilities.

Breaking Internal Walls

To embrace this Spirit of Limitlessness, one must confront the internal walls that life, religion, and trauma often build.

- **Fear** is one such wall. Fear convinces you to stay small. It says, *"Don't dream too big," "Don't step out,"* or *"What if you fail?"* But faith says, *"If God be for us, who can be against us?"* (Romans 8:31). When fear meets faith in the heart of a Spirit-filled believer, fear must bow. Fear cannot exist in the same space where God's perfect love reigns (1 John 4:18).

- **Self-doubt** is another wall. Many are trapped not by external forces but by internal hesitations. They disqualify themselves from greatness because of their past or their perceived inadequacies. But Scripture is filled with imperfect people through whom God expressed His perfect plan. *Moses had a speech problem. David had a scandalous past. Paul had a history of violence.* Yet each of them became conduits of the limitless Kingdom because they allowed God to redefine their limits.

The Spirit of Limitlessness is not interested in preserving your comfort. He is interested in *expanding your capacity.* This is why God will often lead His people into uncomfortable places; wildernesses, battles, and stretches of faith.

Not to punish them, but to prepare them for greater realms of influence. Enlargement never happens in ease. It happens in surrender.

Borderless Vision

Borderless living also requires *borderless vision.* Proverbs 29:18 says, *"Where there is no vision, the people perish."* Vision is the vehicle of expansion. The Spirit of God speaks in pictures, promises, and prophetic glimpses of what could be. The more you see in the Spirit, the more your life aligns with Heaven's limitless supply.

You were never meant to merely *survive.* You were meant to *subdue, multiply, and occupy territory*; spiritually, mentally, economically, and relationally.

This is why Jesus constantly taught about the Kingdom in expansive terms. He compared it to:

- *A mustard seed that grows into a tree,*
- *Leaven that spreads through dough,*
- *A net that gathers many kinds of fish.*

Each of these images point to *growth, spread, and transformation.* The Kingdom never stays where it starts. It is destined to *increase* (Isaiah 9:7).

Prayer: The Limitless Channel

One of the greatest evidences of the Spirit's limitlessness is found in prayer. A praying believer taps into dimensions far beyond natural constraints. Prayer is not just communication; it is *collaboration with God's infinite power.* James 5:16 declares that *"the effectual fervent prayer of a righteous man availeth much."*

That means prayer is *quantum, borderless, and effective.* It crosses time zones, breaks generational curses, and unlocks destinies.

Transformation and Creativity

But limitlessness is not only about expansion, it is also about *transformation.* The Spirit doesn't just take you far—He takes you deep. He breaks through the walls of shame, guilt, and emotional trauma that limit our expression of God's glory.

The Spirit of Limitlessness also empowers *creativity.* The borderless believer doesn't just copy what exists; they birth what has never been seen before. The anointing breeds *innovation.* It turns fishermen into apostles, shepherds into kings, slaves into deliverers. With the Holy Spirit, there is no ceiling. There is only *ever-increasing glory* (2 Corinthians 3:18).

Generational Thinking

This mindset also breeds *generational thinking.* A borderless believer does not think only of what they can achieve in a lifetime, they build *legacies.* They lay foundations for others to walk further and faster.

- *Like Abraham, they believe for blessings that extend beyond their years.*

- *Like David, they gather resources for Solomon's temple.*

- *Like Paul, they write letters that will shape the Church for millennia.*

The Spirit of Limitlessness stretches time itself and embeds eternity into every act of faith.

The Person of Limitlessness

In the end, the Spirit of Limitlessness is not an idea, it is a *Person*. The Holy Spirit is the divine breath of God, active and alive within us.

- When He is welcomed, *limits dissolve.*
- When He is obeyed, *boundaries break.*
- When He is grieved, *expansion halts.*

The key to living a borderless life is *intimacy with this Spirit*. Walk with Him. Listen to Him. Yield to Him.

And you will find that the same Spirit who raised Christ from the dead is the Spirit who will raise your potential from the dust of limitation and seat you in the heavens; *free, fearless, and limitless.*

Borderless Kingdom

Part 1
Let's Go Quantum

"Faith is the quantum leap between the seen and the unseen. Step beyond the limits of logic, and watch God move in infinite possibilities."

Chapter 14
Unlocking The Dynamics Of Subatomic Faith

We are living in a time when the boundaries between science and spirituality are no longer rigid walls but permeable thresholds. What was once seen as the exclusive domain of physicists in white lab coats is now being rediscovered through the lens of faith and divine revelation. Quantum mechanics, the study of the smallest building blocks of matter, has shaken the foundations of classical science with its strange, counterintuitive, and mysterious discoveries.

Particles that appear and disappear, objects that exist in multiple states at once, invisible entanglements across vast distances, these phenomena are not just scientific curiosities; they are windows into a deeper reality. That reality aligns more closely with the language of Scripture than many may realize.

The Bible has always spoken the language of the unseen.

"By faith we understand that the worlds were framed by the word of God, so that the things which are seen were not made of things which are visible" (Hebrews 11:3).

Long before quantum physicists probed the invisible particles of the universe, the Spirit inspired writers to record that reality is governed by unseen forces. Faith, like quantum energy, moves through dimensions that defy human understanding and yet shape all that is material. The Kingdom of God, at its core, is a quantum realm, a spiritual dimension of intelligence, power, and presence that transcends time, space, and matter.

To live in a borderless Kingdom, we must embrace the paradoxes of the Spirit. Just as a subatomic particle can be in multiple places at once, the believer is both seated in heavenly places and walking in earthly shoes. Just as quantum entanglement allows particles to remain connected across time and space, the believer is spiritually entangled with Christ, with the saints of all generations, and with the mission of heaven itself. These are not poetic metaphors; they are spiritual truths more aligned with modern quantum discoveries than with classical Newtonian predictability.

In everyday life, we are surrounded by visible outcomes yet ruled by invisible laws. Gravity, electricity, magnetism, all unseen forces, govern our movement and communication. So too does faith. Faith is the invisible force that accesses divine outcomes. It is the *subatomic energy of the spirit realm*.

Jesus said, *"Whatever you ask in prayer, believe that you have received it, and it will be yours"* (Mark 11:24). That is a spiritual law operating much like quantum observation—belief changes the outcome.

***

But this chapter is not merely an attempt to baptize science into Scripture. It is a call to awaken to the majesty of divine intelligence. God is not merely a religious figure. He is the Master Architect of every known and unknown force in the cosmos. He is the God of gravity and galaxies, the Creator of quarks and quasars. To walk with God is not to abandon science but to transcend it. To walk by faith is not to reject reason but to submit reason to revelation.

The more we understand quantum mechanics, the more we grasp how much of the universe is not under our control, yet still responds to focus, intention, and belief. That is the essence of prayer. That is the core of prophetic decree. That is the spirit of worship. When the believer speaks in faith, they do not merely express emotion, they collapse unseen waves of divine potential into visible form. They alter the atmosphere, bend the trajectory of events, and partner with God to shape destiny.

The Church must begin to think and live *quantumly*. No longer can we afford linear thinking, religious programming, or empirical faith limited by what the eye can see. We must learn to operate on frequencies of Spirit, waves of intercession, and entanglements of destiny. We must train ourselves to sense and steward the invisible, not as mysticism, but as the *mind of Christ*.

As we move through this chapter, we will explore several key principles of quantum theory and their stunning parallels to spiritual life: duality, entanglement, superposition, tunneling, and more. We will see how believers, like subatomic particles, exist in states of divine possibility, and how the Kingdom operates as a field of boundless energy ready to respond to our faith.

The call of the Borderless Kingdom is a call to live from the inside out, from the Spirit outward, not from the flesh inward. Quantum mechanics is not the source of these truths; it is simply the scientific echo of what the Spirit has already declared. Now is the time to align our lives with that echo, not as a science experiment, but as a supernatural lifestyle.

In this era, God is raising up a generation of *spiritual physicists*, men and women who move in the Spirit with the accuracy of a laser and the unpredictability of light. They are not random, but they are free. They are not chaotic, but they are dynamic. They understand that the invisible is not imaginary, and that the energy of faith is more real than matter. These are the borderless ones, the believers who, like Christ, defy the limitations of time, space, and fear.

Welcome to the quantum spirit life—where the Kingdom does not always make sense, but it always makes reality.

Quantum Particles and the Mystery of Duality

One of the most fascinating discoveries in quantum mechanics is the *wave-particle duality* of subatomic particles. This principle reveals that light and matter, traditionally understood as particles can also behave like waves, depending on how they are observed. In classical physics, an object is either a wave or a particle. But in the quantum realm, this boundary dissolves.

Light, for instance, behaves like a wave when not being measured, spreading across space in rippling patterns. Yet when it is observed or measured, it takes on the form of a particle—concentrated and discrete. The implications are profound: matter exists in multiple forms simultaneously, and it chooses its form based on how it is perceived.

This strange property, confirmed by experiments such as the *double-slit test*, has shaken the very foundations of modern science. It suggests that observation itself can affect reality. Even more astounding is how closely this mirrors spiritual truth. The Bible teaches that believers are citizens of two realms at once, both physical and spiritual.

Paul wrote: *"And God raised us up with Christ and seated us with him in the heavenly realms in Christ Jesus"* (Ephesians 2:6). Yet at the same time, we walk and live on earth. This dual existence defies classical logic, but quantum duality provides a powerful framework to understand it.

As quantum particles are both wave and particle, believers are both temporal and eternal, natural and spiritual. They live in physical bodies, yet their spirits are anchored in eternity. Just as an electron exists as a field of probabilities until measured, the believer holds vast spiritual potential that becomes reality when activated by faith and divine alignment. Until a believer comes under God's observation, their full identity remains potential rather than manifestation.

This dual identity is not contradiction; it is divine design. Jesus Himself embodied this mystery. He walked among men, eating, sleeping, weeping, and dying. Yet He also transfigured in glory, walked on water, calmed storms, and rose from the grave. He was fully man and fully God. Just as light behaves as both wave and particle, Jesus bridged heaven and earth in perfect duality.

Scripture confirms: *"As He is, so are we in this world"* (1 John 4:17). This means we too are designed to live as multi-dimensional beings, with access to both spiritual and physical authority.

For too long, the Church has lived as though it were only a "particle"; fixed, predictable, and confined by the laws of physical reality. But God is calling us to embrace our *wave function*; our expansive, flowing, and supernatural nature. Waves cannot be contained. They pass through walls, move beyond borders, and carry power into places particles cannot reach. This is the Spirit-led life: not confined to rituals or regions, but moving with divine fluidity. As Jesus taught: *"The wind blows where it wishes… so it is with everyone born of the Spirit"* (John 3:8). To live a borderless life, we must become more wave than particle, more Spirit than structure.

This revelation reshapes how we see ourselves, our destiny, and our spiritual operations. You are not limited to one expression, one calling, or one identity. Like a quantum particle, your spiritual identity is multi-layered, dynamic, and responsive to divine purpose. You are worshiper, warrior, king, priest, builder, and reformer, all at once. And just as a wave collapses into a particle when observed, you manifest whatever God reveals you to be in the moment. This is why prophetic encounters are so transformative; they align your "wave self" into a focused purpose. You become what heaven sees in you.

Moreover, this duality empowers prayer and intercession. When you pray, you do not speak as a mere human, you speak as an interdimensional ambassador, releasing heavenly reality into earthly conditions. You function in both realms simultaneously. Like waves of energy interacting with matter, your prayers release vibrations that alter circumstances. As James 5:16 declares: *"The prayer of a righteous person is powerful and effective."* The righteous are those aligned in both spirit and body, releasing spiritual energy into earthly systems.

Understanding duality also shatters the illusion of separation. Too often, we compartmentalize life, spiritual on Sunday, natural on Monday. But true Kingdom living is fully integrated: *every business meeting is a mission field, every grocery run a potential healing encounter, every conversation a prophetic opportunity.* The more we embrace this dual nature, the greater our authority. When we acknowledge we are both priests and kings, both human and divine representatives, we shift atmospheres and break barriers.

In quantum mechanics, a particle's state remains undefined until observed. Likewise, many believers live in uncertainty, not for lack of potential, but for lack of divine observation. When God looks upon a person and calls them by name, competing possibilities collapse, and destiny is established.

This is the power of divine calling. Just as Jesus declared over Simon: *"You are Peter, and on this rock, I will build my church"* (Matthew 16:18), so God speaks into us, defining our true form.

At the same time, the enemy also seeks to "measure" us through a fallen lens, limiting us with reminders of past failures, weaknesses, and generational bondage. But when we align with God's gaze, the gaze of grace, identity, and purpose, every false identity collapses, and truth emerges. The battle of faith is not to become something new, but to *agree with how heaven already sees us.*

Wave-particle duality teaches us to live both visible and invisible, practical and prophetic, grounded and glorious. It trains us to move seamlessly between the sacred and the secular, carrying divine essence into everyday life. The natural person seeks a single label; pastor, entrepreneur, parent, or artist. But the Spirit-filled person flows between roles, knowing that each is only a fraction of their eternal identity.

The duality of quantum particles is not a flaw of science; it is a whisper of divinity. The universe itself bears the Creator's signature: paradox, mystery, and majesty. And as those made in His image, we too are paradoxes, weak yet powerful, seen yet unseen, mortal yet eternal. This is the mystery of the *quantum spirit life*. This is the essence of the borderless Kingdom, where we are no longer bound by fixed definitions, but flow in and out of divine function like the very particles that make up the stars.

The Observer Effect: Consciousness Changes Reality

Among the many remarkable phenomena in quantum physics, *the observer effect* may be the most spiritually provocative. This principle states that the very act of observing a quantum system affects the behavior of the particles being observed. A particle can exist in multiple potential states, called a *superposition*, until it is measured. Once observed, it suddenly "collapses" into one specific state. The observer, then, is not passive but active in shaping the outcome. In the quantum world, observation is not neutral, it is creative.

This truth mirrors one of the most foundational principles of spiritual life: *what you focus on shapes your reality.* Scripture emphasizes this repeatedly. *"As a man thinks in his heart, so is he"* (Proverbs 23:7). What we hold in our consciousness, what we choose to observe mentally and spiritually, begins to manifest in the natural. Faith is not passive belief; it is focused vision. It is spiritual observation that transforms unseen possibilities into tangible outcomes.

The observer effect sheds light on why Jesus emphasized guarding the heart and renewing the mind. Our spiritual observation, how we see ourselves, others, and the world, does not merely reflect reality; it influences it. *"The eye is the lamp of the body. If your eyes are healthy, your whole body will be full of light"* (Matthew 6:22–23). Here, "the eye" is not just physical sight but inner vision; the faith filter, the prophetic lens. When your inner gaze aligns with heaven, your entire life becomes illuminated with clarity and power.

Consider the twelve spies sent into Canaan (Numbers 13). They all observed the same land, yet ten saw defeat while only two, Joshua and Caleb; saw promise. The ten, consumed by fear, described themselves as grasshoppers before giants. Their observation collapsed their destiny into defeat. Joshua and Caleb, however, maintained a faith-filled vision, and decades later, they entered the land. This is the observer effect in action: perception shaping reality.

This is the essence of prophetic vision. When believers see as God sees and agree with it, that vision begins to shape external outcomes. In the quantum world, the future is a field of potential. Likewise, in the Spirit, your life is not fixed—it is a divine possibility awaiting the observation of faith. What you *declare, imagine, and believe* matters deeply. Jesus affirmed this: *"Whatever you ask in prayer, believe that you have received it, and it will be yours"* (Mark 11:24). Faith is spiritual measurement; it collapses the unseen into focus.

In prayer, the observer effect is always at work. When we pray according to God's will, we are not merely speaking, we are focusing spiritual energy into specific outcomes. Romans 4:17 speaks of God *"who gives life to the dead and calls things that are not as though they were."* Prayer aligns our vision with God's eternal observation. When we declare healing, freedom, or breakthrough, we are observing in the Spirit what will later manifest in the natural.

But the observer effect also comes with a warning. If our focus is on fear, defeat, or failure, we risk collapsing our lives into those very outcomes. Worry is negative observation. Fear is corrupted focus. Both empower darkness by aligning with impossibility. That is why Scripture instructs: *"Fix our eyes not on what is seen, but on what is unseen"* (2 Corinthians 4:18). Only when we anchor our gaze in eternity do we step into the flow of supernatural outcomes.

We see this principle perfectly embodied in Jesus. He looked at Simon the fisherman and observed Peter the rock. He looked at the woman caught in adultery and observed a restored daughter. He looked at Zacchaeus the tax collector and observed a transformed man. Jesus changed people by how He saw them. His divine observation collapsed shame and failure into destiny.

This same call rests on every believer: to see with the eyes of Christ. To observe not only what is, but what *could be.* To move from natural sight to spiritual insight. This transforms not only our own lives but the lives of others. Prophecy is simply the advanced form of the observer effect, it is seeing what heaven sees and declaring it until it manifests.

In leadership, this principle becomes a tool for empowerment. Great leaders don't just manage people; they shape realities. By focusing on potential rather than weakness, they become mirrors through which people see their true selves. Kingdom leaders magnify destiny, not immaturity.

In worship, the observer effect lifts our eyes above circumstances and fixes them on God. *"As we behold Him, we are transformed"* (2 Corinthians 3:18). Worship is spiritual observation; it aligns our inner vision with God's reality until glory collapses into our brokenness.

***

The observer effect reveals that consciousness is not neutral, it is a shaping force. Faith-filled observation partners with heaven, while fear-filled observation partners with defeat. As citizens of a borderless Kingdom, we are called to be intentional observers: fixing our eyes on the unseen, declaring what God declares, and shaping reality through vision. The Kingdom expands not only through action, but also through focus. What you see is what you manifest.

***

Quantum Entanglement: Instant Connection Beyond Distance

In the captivating world of quantum mechanics, one of the most mystifying phenomena is *quantum entanglement*. This principle describes how two particles, once connected, remain in deep, unbreakable correlation no matter how far apart they are. Change the state of one, and the other instantly responds, even if separated by light-years. This occurs faster than the speed of light, defying traditional laws of locality and space-time. Einstein called it *"spooky action at a distance."* Yet, despite its mystery, entanglement is scientifically proven and experimentally validated.

Now imagine the spiritual implications. What if our spirits, once joined to Christ, become entangled with Him in such a way that no distance; spatial, emotional, or spiritual, can sever that connection? This is not hypothetical; it is the truth of Scripture. *"Whoever is united with the Lord is one with Him in spirit"* (1 Corinthians 6:17).

When a person receives Christ, a divine fusion occurs. You are no longer isolated; you are intertwined with the Spirit of God in an indivisible bond.

This principle explains why the believer can access the *mind of Christ* (1 Corinthians 2:16), receive spiritual downloads, experience prophetic dreams, and be led by the Spirit in real time. It also explains how intercession works. When you pray for someone across the world, your words, fueled by love and Spirit, pierce distance and touch their life immediately. It is not sympathy; it is *spiritual entanglement.* Believers are part of one body, one Spirit, one eternal system.

Jesus prayed for this in John 17:21: *"That all of them may be one, Father, just as You are in Me and I am in You."* This was not organizational unity but entangled oneness; supernatural, indivisible connection. Just as entangled particles act in tandem regardless of distance, believers spiritually entangled with Christ and each other move in synchronized power.

In this Kingdom, distance does not weaken influence. You may be absent physically but present spiritually. Paul expressed this to the Colossians: *"Though I am absent in the body, I am present with you in spirit"* (Colossians 2:5). He operated from a quantum level of spiritual connection. Prayer warriors, prophets, and apostolic leaders still govern regions they never physically occupy, connected through divine entanglement.

This also explains the weight of covenant relationships. When God joins two people; whether in marriage, friendship, or ministry; He forges a bond that transcends time and location. Ruth and Naomi, David and Jonathan, Paul and Timothy; all bore fruit far beyond their time together. To betray such a bond is to break an entangled cord. To remain loyal preserves its integrity and multiplies its impact.

In intercession, entanglement creates burdens of the Spirit. You suddenly feel compelled to pray for someone you have not seen in years. This is not sentiment, it is *spiritual data* moving through the quantum field of prayer. Your obedience may shift outcomes you never witness, yet heaven records the effect.

Even the *communion of saints* is a type of entanglement. Hebrews 12:1 says we are *"surrounded by a great cloud of witnesses."* They are not absent but entangled. Heaven and earth are interconnected dimensions. Revelation 8:4 shows the prayers of the saints rising and mingling with heavenly incense before God. What we pray here stirs action there.

On a personal level, this truth reshapes our perspective. You are not an isolated individual but part of a vast, invisible network of divine purpose. *Your obedience matters. Your purity matters. Your worship matters.* The success of one believer strengthens the faith of many. The fall of one reverberates far beyond themselves. Such is the gravity of entanglement.

This principle also comforts us. When you feel forgotten, you are remembered. When you pray in secret, your voice touches eternal dimensions. The borderless Kingdom ensures you are always connected. God's Spirit in you is entangled with His will and power. That means His peace can reach your anxiety in an instant, His healing can flow to your pain without delay, and His voice can pierce your doubt faster than light.

Entanglement reveals a vital truth: in the Kingdom, *proximity is spiritual, not spatial.* What you are aligned with spiritually influences you more than what surrounds you physically. You can sit in a crowded church and feel far away, or pray alone in your room and feel overwhelmed by God's nearness. Your entanglement determines your experience.

This carries profound implications for revival and transformation. The next move of God will not be contained by buildings or nations. It will be carried by entangled believers, connected in prayer, united in purpose, synchronized by the Spirit. Their agreement will transcend language. Their love will outpace travel. Their fire will leap continents, carried not by programs but by spiritual connection.

***

Quantum entanglement teaches that relationship in the Spirit is not mere fellowship—it is fusion. We are bonded with Christ, with each other, and with the Kingdom. That bond is eternal, invisible, unbreakable. It empowers intercession, fuels mission, sustains faith, and releases glory. To live in this awareness is to live in the quantum life of the borderless Kingdom.

***

Superposition: Holding Multiple Potentials at Once

In quantum physics, one of the most fascinating concepts is *superposition*. A quantum particle can exist in multiple states at once until it is measured, an electron spinning both up and down, or a photon traveling multiple paths simultaneously. It defies linear logic yet is scientifically verified.

Now consider this truth spiritually. Superposition is not limited to particles; it is a mirror of the multi-dimensional identity of every believer. You are not *one thing*—you are *many things*. You are a child of God, an heir of promise, a warrior, a worshiper, a builder, and a carrier of Kingdom

DNA. All coexist within you, even if only one is visible at a time. Your spirit holds *superpositioned destiny*—layers of calling and creativity awaiting revelation.

The world defines identity in single dimensions: *"You are a teacher," "You are a mother," "You are a businessperson."* But in the borderless Kingdom, your calling is not reduced to what is seen. You may run a business while carrying a revival anointing. You may serve in obscurity while training as an apostolic pioneer. Heaven sees your full spectrum, even when earth sees only fragments.

Scripture illustrates this beautifully. David was shepherd, warrior, musician, and king. Even while tending sheep, he carried royal anointing. Joseph was dreamer, slave, prisoner, and ruler. His palace identity existed in the pit. Jesus Himself is the ultimate picture of divine superposition, the Lamb and the Lion, the Servant and the King, the Son of Man and the Son of God. Multiple realities coexisted in Him at every moment.

This is the revelation the Church must reclaim. Too many believers live trapped by the visible, unaware of the unseen dimensions within them. Like a particle in superposition, your life holds divine options, possibilities waiting for faith to collapse them into reality. Prophetic ministry plays a crucial role here: a prophet peers into your superposition and names what has not yet appeared. They see the king in the shepherd, the preacher in the prisoner, the deliverer in the stutterer. When that word is received, potential collapses into purpose.

Superposition also reminds us of divine patience. Delay is not denial. Abraham was called father of nations while childless. Sarah laughed because she could not reconcile the visible with the invisible. But God speaks from superposition, declaring the end from the beginning.

It also transforms how we see others. The addicted man may be an apostle in waiting. The rebellious teen may be a prophet in disguise. Our role is not to freeze people in their present measurement but to call forth their unseen identity.

Practically, this means holding space for divine ambiguity. Being in transition does not mean being off track, it may mean multiple possibilities are being held in tension until obedience reveals the way. It also means embracing seasons of multiplicity: raising children while leading nations, building a business while planting a church, walking through therapy while carrying revival. These are not contradictions but expressions of multifaceted calling.

Superposition declares that limitation is perception, not reality. You are never "just" anything. You are filled with potential waiting for faith's observation. To live a super positioned life is to walk in wonder, knowing God can unveil a new layer of your calling at any moment. This is not instability but divine flexibility.

***

Superposition teaches that borderless living means borderless identity. You are not confined to what you were or even to what you are. You are filled with what you could become. Every act of faith collapses potential into reality. You are a divine composite, a walking paradox, a living mystery. Welcome to the quantum life of the Kingdom.

Part 2

Let's Go Quantum

Collapsing the Wave Function: Decision as Destiny

The unseen is never empty; it is alive with possibility. Step into the quantum of faith, and watch the invisible shape the visible.

Chapter 15

Collapsing the Wave Function: Decision as Destiny

In the quantum world, a phenomenon known as *wave function collapse* occurs when a system, previously existing in a state of multiple probabilities, shifts into a single, definite state due to observation or measurement. Until this point, the particle lives in what physicists call *superposition*; a realm of all possible outcomes. But the moment it is measured, the wave of possibilities collapses into one reality.

The act of observing doesn't merely reveal the state, it defines it. *Measurement births manifestation.*

This principle reflects a profound spiritual truth: life's outcomes are not determined merely by potential, but by decision. Destiny is not automatic; it is summoned through choices. As God declares in Deuteronomy 30:19:

"I have set before you life and death, blessings and curses. Now choose life, so that you and your children may live."

The divine invitation is not passive, it is proactive. The power to collapse potential into purpose is entrusted to every believer. You are not the product of fate; you are the product of decisions.

Faith as the Measuring Device

Just as in quantum mechanics, your life holds multiple potential outcomes. Every gift, prophecy, and opportunity carries within it a range of possible futures. Which one becomes reality depends on how you *see, believe, and act*.

In the spirit-realm, *faith is the measuring device* that collapses God's promises into personal experience. Until faith is engaged, potential remains suspended. This is why James 2:17 insists: *"Faith without works is dead."*

Without corresponding action, observation never collapses into reality.

Biblical Portraits of Collapse

- **Abraham** was given promises as vast as the stars. Yet they remained possibilities until he *believed* and *obeyed*. Leaving his father's house and being willing to sacrifice Isaac were decisive actions that collapsed God's word into reality. His choices activated the covenant.

- **Peter** stepped out of the boat. Walking on water was only a possibility until his movement collapsed it into miracle.

- **The woman with the issue of blood** touched Jesus' garment. Her decision was more than hope, it was measurement. Her faith pulled healing from atmosphere into her body.

Faith is never passive. It is decisive agreement with divine potential.

The Danger of Passivity

In today's Church, many hear prophetic words, absorb teaching, and collect revelation, yet never collapse them into tangible change. They float in endless possibility without action. This creates spiritual frustration: full of knowledge, but empty in experience.

Why?

Because *what is heard must be measured*. Revelation without obedience remains theoretical. In quantum faith, neutrality is not safety, it is paralysis. Heaven responds to movement.

When God says "go," staying still becomes disobedience. When He says "speak," silence becomes resistance. Every act of obedience measures the unseen and manifests the miraculous.

Decision as Destiny

Mary's response to Gabriel; *"Let it be unto me according to your word"*—was the moment divine seed took root.

Her agreement collapsed the promise into incarnation. Her destiny was not inevitable, it was embraced.

This reveals the weight of *daily choices*. To pray or not. To forgive or not. To sow or not. Each decision is a collapsing point, sealing a version of reality. Scripture urges us to walk in wisdom and be led by the Spirit because every decision steers destiny.

Collapse Requires Congruence

It is not enough to *declare* faith without *deciding* faith. Too many believers say "breakthrough" while living in bitterness, or proclaim "harvest" while practicing procrastination. This inconsistency breeds confusion.

Collapse requires congruence, alignment between confession and action.

To walk in the Spirit is to bring unity between what you speak, what you believe, and what you do.

Leadership and Wave Collapse

In leadership, this principle is magnified. Leaders must not only carry vision; they must make decisions that collapse vision into culture.

- *Vision without execution is spiritual superposition, full of potential but lacking substance.*

- *But when Spirit-led leaders decide boldly, atmospheres shift, momentum builds, and destiny unfolds.*

Decisive leadership, bathed in prayer and humility, becomes the collapsing point for communities and movements.

Freedom from Perfectionism

Wave collapse is not about perfection, it's about *decision*. A quantum particle does not wait for perfect conditions. Likewise, God is not waiting for you to be flawless. He is waiting for your *yes*.

When you move, even imperfectly, grace fills the gaps. Heaven honors motion. This frees us from paralysis by analysis. You can stumble into obedience, fail forward, and still collapse destiny into manifestation.

Borderless Collapse

In a borderless Kingdom, collapse applies everywhere. Decisions in business, education, politics, or family are as spiritual as those made in church. Every act of obedience, whether hiring staff, forgiving an offense, or raising children, becomes a measurement that brings heaven into earth's systems.

Kingdom living is holistic. *Every platform is a pulpit.* Every obedient act is a wave collapse for Kingdom culture.

***

*The collapse of the wave function reminds us that **decisions shape destiny**. God has set before you, infinite spiritual potential. His promises are yes—but your agreement is the amen.*

Your decision brings definition. Your obedience makes miracles manifest. You are not a prisoner of chance— you are a co-creator with Christ. Every time you say yes to God, something collapses into glory.

And in that collapse, destiny is not just revealed—it is fulfilled.

***

Quantum Tunneling and Breaking Through Barriers

One of the most astonishing and counterintuitive phenomena in quantum physics is known as *quantum tunneling*. In classical physics, a particle can only move past a barrier if it has enough energy to overcome it. But in quantum physics, subatomic particles routinely pass through barriers that should be impassable. They literally *tunnel* through walls without breaking them or climbing over.

It defies logic, violates classical rules, and exposes the weakness of linear limitations. Where physics says, *"This is impossible,"* quantum tunneling whispers, *"There is another way."*

Spiritual Tunneling

This principle is not just a scientific curiosity; it is a profound metaphor for the way God moves in the lives of His people. In the natural world, many situations are labeled hopeless. Logic, probability, or human experience declare there is no way forward. Yet the Kingdom of God does not operate on classical rules. It moves in the realm of *quantum grace*, where what should block you becomes passable through divine intervention.

The Spirit enables believers to tunnel through walls, break through ceilings, and defy expectations.

Scripture is full of such moments, *spiritual tunneling* where barriers dissolved before God's power:

- **The Red Sea** opened, making way for Israel when both geography and enemy armies declared defeat. What looked like a trap became a birth canal for a nation.

- **Daniel in the lions' den, Jonah in the fish, Jericho's collapsing walls, Paul and Silas in**

prison—all were impossible barriers that became supernatural exits.

The impossibility became the testimony.

The Language of Tunneling

Zechariah 4:6–7 declares:

"Not by might, nor by power, but by my Spirit, says the Lord… What are you, O great mountain? Before Zerubbabel, you shall become a plain!"

This is tunneling language. The Spirit bypasses brute force and opens invisible doors. The *borderless Kingdom* does not depend on favorable conditions. It thrives on faith's energy. Where flesh sees walls, the Spirit sees portals.

Implications for the Believer

There will be seasons where logic says, *"You cannot pass."* The degree is insufficient. The resources are lacking. The system is rigged. The diagnosis is final.

But in those very moments, if you remain sensitive to the Spirit, you will feel His current pulling you forward. This is the tunneling power of God. He leads through closed doors without keys. He moves you through impossible places without the world's resources.

Resistance is not a verdict; it is an invitation. In quantum mechanics, barriers are thresholds waiting for the right energy. In the Spirit, that energy is called *faith, obedience, and divine momentum.* When these converge, barriers become opportunities for God's glory to be revealed.

Jesus, the Ultimate Tunnel

Jesus modeled this reality. He walked through locked doors to reach His disciples (John 20:26). He passed through angry crowds untouched. He raised the dead, bypassing the supposed finality of death.

The *resurrection itself* was the greatest quantum tunnel. The stone was real, the guards were real, the tomb was sealed, and yet Jesus emerged in power. Death was the ultimate wall, but *grace was the greater force.*

As heirs with Christ, we are called to move with the same expectation. We do not face walls like the world does. We carry within us the tunneling Spirit of God, who specializes in breakthroughs that defy reason.

The Call to Expectation

When you hit a wall in ministry, business, health, or family, your first instinct should not be despair, it should be *expectation.*

Ask the Spirit: *"Where is the tunnel?"*

Trust that what is impassable in the natural is navigable in the supernatural.

This requires discernment. Not every wall is meant to be broken, some are designed to be passed through. God's strategies are unconventional.

A job that looks like a step backward may be a tunnel into influence. A delayed promotion may be the setup for accelerated breakthrough. Generosity in lean times may become the hidden gateway to abundance.

These are not detours. They are divine corridors disguised as limitations.

The Mystery of Progress

Tunneling also demands trust. Passing through barriers often means moving in low visibility. It can feel like nothing is shifting, even though everything is moving beneath the surface.

That is the mystery of tunneling, you make progress in realms unseen. God is whispering your name in rooms you have never entered, aligning systems on your behalf, and preparing hearts before you arrive. Your obedience initiates unseen momentum.

Psalm 18:29 proclaims: *"By my God, I can leap over a wall."* Sometimes that leap is over. Other times, it is *through*. The truth remains; the wall does not win.

Tunneling Faith and Prayer

Tunneling faith reshapes prayer. You no longer ask merely for hardship to be removed; you pray to find the hidden pathways through it. You believe that even in wilderness there is water, in exile there is favor, in opposition there is access.

You stop praying only for *doors*, you pray for *tunnels*. This is mature faith. It trusts that God will make a way, even when no way is visible.

Tunneling in Leadership

For leaders, tunneling is a kingdom strategy. When institutions resist revival, when politics suppress righteousness, or when culture mocks holiness, we do not retreat. We tunnel.

We plant underground prayer movements. We publish truth in hidden streams. We infiltrate systems with faith-led solutions. Like particles passing through walls, God's people move in unconventional ways to release His will on earth.

***

Quantum tunneling is the divine technology of breakthrough. It bypasses opposition, transcends delay, and manifests outcomes that logic cannot predict.

As citizens of the borderless Kingdom, we are not defined by what stops others. We are empowered by a Spirit who specializes in tunneling through.

So do not fear the wall. Ask for the tunnel. Trust the invisible path. Keep moving until the obstacle becomes evidence of supernatural passage.

The Kingdom is advancing, and it is tunneling through

***.

The Quantum Kingdom: God's Operating System

The Kingdom of God is not just a theological concept; it is a living, dynamic system that governs all creation, visible and invisible. It is an ecosystem of divine order, power, and purpose that transcends time, matter, and space. In essence, it is God's *operating system*, and it functions much like a quantum framework.

While earthly kingdoms rely on hierarchy, geography, and control, the Kingdom of God operates through Spirit, alignment, and revelation. It is designed for expansion, transformation, and limitless connectivity, a truly *borderless reality*.

At the heart of quantum physics is the idea that the universe is not rigid or mechanical but a fluid, interactive field of possibilities, governed by invisible forces and interdependent relationships.

Likewise, the Kingdom is a realm of divine interaction where Spirit governs substance and outcomes are shaped by alignment with the King's will. Here, faith functions as the ultimate interface, allowing believers to participate in divine reality.

Quantum Patterns in Scripture

Jesus constantly taught Kingdom principles that reflect quantum patterns:

- *"The Kingdom of God is within you"* (Luke 17:21) shattered the notion that God's rule is confined to temples or thrones. The Kingdom operates from the inside out.

- **Non-locality:** Like quantum-entangled particles, Kingdom influence transcends geography. A prayer whispered in a closet can shift events across continents (Acts 10: Peter's vision in Joppa).

- **Multiplicity without division:** One revelation, one word, or one act can impact generations without losing its potency. Jesus multiplied five loaves and two fish without diminishing them.

- **Measurement-dependent outcomes:** *"According to your faith, be it unto you"* demonstrates that perception and participation shape experience. The same power produces different results depending on belief.

- **Heart posture matters:** The widow's two coins (Mark 12:41–44) show the Kingdom measures intent over quantity. It honors essence, not appearance.

- **Quantum inheritance**: Romans 8:17 teaches we are co-heirs with Christ, but inheritance is activated by faith, obedience, and alignment, not passively received.

Decentralized and Holographic Kingdom

The Kingdom is decentralized and holographic, much like a quantum network. No single church, ministry, or leader holds the whole. Each believer carries *Kingdom DNA*, expanding God's system wherever they are.

The early Church grew explosively because power was distributed, not centralized. Filled with the Spirit, every believer became a point of ignition, expanding influence from the inside out.

Words are powerful. Proverbs 18:21 reminds us that *"life and death are in the power of the tongue."* Every declaration is a seed, a measurement, and a potential reality. Declarations collapse possibilities into existence.

Obedience is the operating code of the Kingdom. Every instruction from God triggers divine activity. Like quantum tunneling, obedience enables passage through seemingly impossible barriers, unlocking hidden provision, healing, and favor.

Unity amplifies power. John 17 highlights entanglement in agreement: when believers align, influence multiplies. Matthew 18:19 emphasizes that agreement is not additive—it is multiplicative.

Rest is also quantum. Hebrews 4 describes Sabbath-rest as alignment without resistance, where energy flows freely. Miracles happen without strain when your will is fully in sync with God's.

Finally, the quantum Kingdom spans eternity. Like quantum particles, it exists across dimensions.

"The Kingdom is at hand" (Matthew 3:2) reminds us that it is active now. Participation brings influence over angels, nations, and the very fabric of creation.

Living the Quantum Life of the Spirit

To live a quantum life in the Spirit is to live awake, aware, and aligned. It is to operate within God's supernatural operating system with clarity, purpose, and bold faith. This is not reserved for mystics or prophets, it is the birthright of every believer.

- **Consciousness Shift**: Romans 12:2 calls for a renewed mind. Seeing through the lens of Kingdom reality reveals portals instead of barriers, patterns instead of chaos, and possibilities instead of limits.

- **Creative Participation**: Thoughts, words, and choices are creative forces. Every act of obedience collapses possibility into reality. Complaining and passivity are replaced by proactivity, prophecy, and purpose.

- **Sensitivity to the Spirit**: Like quantum systems, small interactions trigger significant outcomes. Divine whispers can reroute destiny and unlock provision. Intimacy with God is essential for quantum living.

- **Faith and Risk**: Faith is bold and dangerous to comfort zones. To move in the Spirit is to say yes before seeing, to give before the harvest, and to believe when everything suggests otherwise. Miracles collapse into moments through courageous steps.

- **Stewardship of Relationships**: Divine connections are entangled with purpose. Discernment is required to honor those aligned with your frequency and release those who drain spiritual energy.

- **Time Alignment**: Time is not linear in the Spirit. Kairos moments allow a single year to accomplish what ten years could not. Discernment ensures alignment with God's timing.

- **Kingdom in Every Sphere**: Vocation, business, and daily responsibilities become portals for Kingdom expansion. The sacred/secular divide collapses; every assignment carries eternal significance.

- **Supernatural Resilience**: Rooted in Spirit frequency, believers tunnel through challenges while others falter. Momentum flows from Spirit-led alignment, not natural effort.

- **Limitless Expansion**: Borderless potential defines quantum living. Faith opens new fields of possibility. You were created to reflect the infinite, invisible design of the Creator.

***

You are a quantum being embedded with divine code. You are entangled with heaven, entrusted with purpose, and empowered by Spirit. You are not random. You are not powerless. You are Spirit-born, Spirit-led, and Spirit-empowered.

Tune your frequency to faith. Measure your steps with obedience. Speak with creative authority. Move boldly through every wall, delay, or system standing in your way.

Welcome to the quantum life of the Kingdom—where all things are possible, and nothing is out of reach.

***

Chapter 16

55 Scriptures on Borderless Living

I. The Call to Expansion and Increase

1. **Genesis 1:28** – *"Be fruitful and multiply; fill the earth and subdue it..."*
   (NKJV)

2. **Isaiah 54:2–3** – *"Enlarge the place of your tent... Your descendants will inherit the nations..."*
   (NIV)

3. **Deuteronomy 11:24** – *"Every place where you set your foot will be yours..."*
   (NIV)

4. **Joshua 1:3** – *"Every place that the sole of your foot will tread upon I have given you..."*
   (ESV)

5. **1 Chronicles 4:10** – *"Oh, that You would bless me indeed, and enlarge my territory..."* **(NKJV)**

6. **Isaiah 60:22** – *"A little one shall become a thousand, and a small one a strong nation..."* **(NKJV)**

7. **Psalm 115:14–15** – *"May the Lord give you increase more and more, you and your children..."* **(NKJV)**

8. **Job 8:7** – *"Though your beginning was small, yet your latter end would increase abundantly."* **(NKJV)**

II. A Kingdom for All Nations

9. **Zechariah 2:4–5** – *"Jerusalem will be a city without walls... I will be a wall of fire around her..."* **(NIV)**

10. **Matthew 28:19–20** – *"Go therefore and make disciples of all nations..."*
    (ESV)

11. **Psalm 2:8** – *"Ask of Me, and I will give You the nations for Your inheritance..."*
    (NKJV)

12. **Revelation 7:9** – *"...a great multitude from every nation, tribe, people and language..."*
    (NIV)

13. **Isaiah 66:18–19** – *"The time is coming to gather all nations and tongues..."*
    (NIV)

14. **Micah 4:1–2** – *"...the mountain of the Lord's house shall be established... and peoples shall flow to it."*
    (ESV)

15. **Isaiah 49:6** – *"...that My salvation may reach to the ends of the earth."*
    (NIV)

16. **Matthew 24:14** – "...this gospel of the kingdom will be preached in the whole world..." **(NIV)**

17. **Colossians 1:6** – "This same Good News... is going out all over the world..." **(NLT)**

18. **Romans 10:18** – "Their sound has gone out to all the earth..." **(NKJV)**

19. **Acts 1:8** – "..you will be My witnesses... to the ends of the earth." **(ESV)**

20. **Acts 2:39** – "...for all who are far off—as many as the Lord our God will call." **(NIV)**

III. Shaking Systems Through Sound and Spirit

21. **Psalm 19:4** – *"Their voice goes out into all the earth..."*
(NIV)

22. **Psalm 147:15** – *"He sends out His command to the earth; His word runs swiftly."*
(NIV)

23. **Isaiah 42:10** – *"Sing to the Lord a new song, His praise from the ends of the earth..."*
(NKJV)

24. **Revelation 11:15** – *"The kingdoms of this world have become the kingdoms of our Lord..."*
(KJV)

25. **Hebrews 12:26–27** – *"...now He has promised, 'Yet once more I shake not only the earth but also the heavens.'"*
(ESV)

26. **Haggai 2:7** – *"I will shake all nations... and I will fill this house with glory..."*
(NIV)

27. **Isaiah 11:9** – *"...the earth shall be full of the knowledge of the Lord..."*
(ESV)

28. **Habakkuk 2:14** – *"...the earth will be filled with the knowledge of the glory of the Lord..."*
(ESV)

IV. Freedom, Identity, and Unity in Christ

29. **Galatians 3:28** – *"There is neither Jew nor Gentile... for you are all one in Christ Jesus."*
(NIV)

30. **Ephesians 2:14** – *"He... has destroyed the barrier, the dividing wall of hostility..."*
(NIV)

31. **2 Corinthians 3:17** – *"Where the Spirit of the Lord is, there is freedom."*
(ESV)

32. **John 3:8** – *"The wind blows wherever it pleases... So it is with everyone born of the Spirit."*
(NIV)

33. **Matthew 5:14** – *"You are the light of the world. A city on a hill cannot be hidden."*
(NIV)

34. **Isaiah 43:19** – *"I am doing a new thing... I will make a way in the wilderness..."*
(ESV)

35. **Proverbs 4:18** – *"The path of the righteous is like the morning sun..."*
(NIV)

36. **Philippians 3:13–14** – *"...Forgetting what is behind... I press on toward the goal..."*
(NIV)

V. Dominion and Spiritual Government

37. **Psalm 24:1** – *"The earth is the Lord's, and everything in it..."*
(KJV)

38. **Daniel 7:14** – *"His dominion is an everlasting dominion..."*
(ESV)

39. **Isaiah 9:7** – *"Of the greatness of His government and peace there will be no end..."*
(NIV)

40. **Luke 14:23** – *"Go out to the roads and country lanes and compel them to come in..."*
(NIV)

41. **Jeremiah 1:10** – *"I appoint you over nations... to uproot and tear down..."*
(NIV)

42. **Isaiah 61:1–2** – *"...to proclaim liberty to the captives and the opening of the prison..."*
(ESV)

43. **Romans 8:19** – *"The creation waits in eager expectation for the children of God..."*
(NIV)

44. **Mark 16:20** – *"And they went out and preached everywhere..."*
(ESV)

45. **Daniel 2:35** – *"...and the stone... became a great mountain and filled the whole earth."*
(NIV)

VI. River, Increase, and Glory Everywhere

46. **Ezekiel 47:9** – *"Wherever the river flows, everything will live."*
(NLT)

47. **Psalm 89:25** – *"I will set his hand also in the sea, and his right hand in the rivers."*
(KJV)

48. **Isaiah 45:2–3** – *"I will go before you... I will give you hidden treasures..."*
(NIV)

49. **Psalm 18:19** – *"He brought me out into a broad place..."*
(ESV)

50. **Isaiah 58:12** – *"Your people will rebuild the ancient ruins..."*
(NIV)

51. **2 Corinthians 10:16** – *"To preach the gospel in the regions beyond you..."*
(ESV)

52. **Matthew 11:12** – *"The kingdom of heaven suffers violence..."*
(KJV)

53. **John 14:12** – *"Whoever believes in Me... will do even greater works..."*
(NIV)

54. **Isaiah 9:6–7** – *"...and the government will be on His shoulders... Of His peace there will be no end."*
(NIV)

55. **Psalm 22:27** – *"All the ends of the world shall remember and turn to the Lord..."*
(KJV)

"Speak them, believe them, live them, these declarations are keys to breaking every boundary and stepping fully into the limitless life God designed for you."

Chapter 17

My Forty Borderless Decrees

Here are 40 powerful decrees of personal borderlessness to be spoken aloud as affirmations of identity, dominion, expansion, and spiritual freedom. These declarations are inspired by the principles of Borderless Kingdom and rooted in Scripture. They are crafted to help individuals break mental, emotional, spiritual, and territorial limitations.

***

1. **I decree and I declare** that I am made in the image of a borderless God; therefore, no limit can define or restrict me.

2. **I decree and I declare** that the Spirit of God lives in me, making me unstoppable, uncontainable, and unshakable.

3. **I decree and I declare** that I am a citizen of Heaven, and I operate under the authority of a Kingdom with no end.

4. **I decree and I declare** that I reflect the likeness of God and represent His presence in every territory I enter.

5. **I decree and I declare** that I carry the divine DNA of Christ—limitless in calling, eternal in value, and destined for greatness.

6. **I decree and I declare** that my identity is not confined by race, culture, geography, or my past—I am who God says I am.

7. **I decree and I declare** that fear, shame, and guilt can no longer draw boundaries around my destiny.

8. **I decree and I declare** that I am a mobile embassy of God's Kingdom, carrying His authority wherever I go.

9. **I decree and I declare** that all religious, traditional, and man-made barriers are broken by my revelation of Christ.

10. **I decree and I declare** that I am filled with God's fire, favor, and fruit, destined to break limits and set new standards.

DECREES FOR THE EXERCISE OF SPIRITUAL AUTHORITY & DOMINION

11. **I decree and I declare** that every place the sole of my foot shall tread is given to me for Kingdom dominion and influence.

12. **I decree and I declare** that I am appointed by God to uproot, destroy, build, and plant in every land He sends me.

13. **I decree and I declare** that I have spiritual jurisdiction over territories and powers through the name of Jesus.

14. **I decree and I declare** that I shift atmospheres, overturn systems, and release Heaven's will on earth.

15. **I decree and I declare** that I do not need human permission to fulfill a divine mandate—I am commissioned by God.

16. **I decree and I declare** that my words are infused with divine authority and release supernatural results.

17. **I decree and I declare** that I possess spiritual keys to unlock access and shut down opposition.

18. **I decree and I declare** that my hands are blessed to build, prosper, and produce in every season.

19. **I decree and I declare** that my gifts make room for me globally and bring me before decision-makers and kings.

20. **I decree and I declare** that I move in apostolic boldness, prophetic accuracy, and Kingdom insight.

DECREES FOR EXPANSION & INFLUENCE

21. **I decree and I declare** that I am expanding in all directions—spiritually, mentally, financially, and territorially.

22. **I decree and I declare** that boundary lines fall in pleasant places for me; I step fully into my inheritance.

23. **I decree and I declare** that my vision and assignment are global in scope and eternal in impact.

24. **I decree and I declare** that I carry innovative ideas, healing words, and divine strategies for nations.

25. **I decree and I declare** that I am the generation breaker and curse breaker in my bloodline.

26. **I decree and I declare** that no system, label, or ceiling can stop what God has ordained for my life.

27. **I decree and I declare** that I increase daily in wisdom, stature, favor, and credibility.

28. **I decree and I declare** that divine acceleration moves me beyond human timelines and delays.

29. **I decree and I declare** that I rise with clarity, courage, and confidence to take new territory.

30. **I decree and I declare** that my voice, presence, and work will have influence beyond borders.

DECREES FOR FREEDOM & MOVEMENT

31. **I decree and I declare** that I move like the wind—unpredictable to man, but governed by the Spirit of God.

32. **I decree and I declare** that no wall, system, or culture can cage my divine calling.

33. **I decree and I declare** that every invisible prison holding my destiny is now shattered by God's power.

34. **I decree and I declare** that I will not be bound by time, geography, or human approval—I follow God's command.

35. **I decree and I declare** that I am delivered from all generational curses, ceilings, and limitations.

36. **I decree and I declare** that I live by divine rhythm—never rushed by fear, nor paralyzed by doubt.

37. **I decree and I declare** that I am moved by the wind of revival and powered by the breath of God.

38. **I decree and I declare** that open doors and divine gates usher me into my new realms of influence.

39. **I decree and I declare** that my life and legacy will cross borders, heal cultures, and glorify God.

40. **I decree and I declare** that I will live, move, and reign without borders—fully yielded to the King of Glory.

Chapter 18

A 7-Day Borderless Devotional

Day 1: The Call to Expansion

Theme: *God is not limited by our constraints; He's committed to our enlargement.*

Key Scripture: *"Enlarge the place of your tent..."* — *Isaiah 54:2–3*

Devotional:
God's Kingdom is inherently expansive. From creation, His command to humanity was clear: be fruitful, multiply, and take dominion. He has always sought to enlarge His people's capacity—spiritually, emotionally, and geographically. When God instructed Israel to stretch their tent pegs, He was speaking not only of land but also of mindset. A borderless believer prepares for increase even before it manifests.

Scriptures to Meditate On:

- *Genesis 1:28*

- *Isaiah 54:2–3*

- *Deuteronomy 11:24*

- *1 Chronicles 4:10*

Prayer Point:

Lord, stretch my vision and increase my capacity. Help me make room for all You have planned.

Day 2: Possessing the Nations

Theme: *The Kingdom is global, and so is your inheritance.*

Key Scripture: *"Ask of Me, and I will give You the nations..."* —Psalm 2:8

Devotional:

God's heart is for the nations. He chose Israel to be a light to the Gentiles, and Christ confirmed this with the Great Commission. The Kingdom is not local—it is global. As co-heirs with Christ, we are empowered to impact regions, disciple cultures, and influence systems. Spiritually, there are no language barriers or closed doors. Your influence is not limited by your location.

Scriptures to Meditate On:

- *Psalm 2:8*
- *Matthew 28:19–20*
- *Revelation 7:9*

- *Isaiah 49:6*

Prayer Point:

Father, give me a heart for the nations. Break every limiting belief that tells me I cannot go further.

Day 3: Shaking Systems Through Sound

Theme: *Heaven's sound shakes earthly systems.*

Key Scripture: *"At that time His voice shook the earth..." —Hebrews 12:26–27*

Devotional:

God often uses sound to precede movement. From creation to Pentecost, sound marked divine transitions. The sound of worship, intercession, and prophetic declaration carries authority to shake systems. As a borderless believer, your voice has power—not through volume, but alignment with Heaven's frequency. Your agreement with God's Word has global impact.

Scriptures to Meditate On:

- *Hebrews 12:26–27*

- *Psalm 19:4*
- *Acts 1:8*
- *Haggai 2:7*

Prayer Point:

Lord, let my voice echo Your truth. Use me to release sound that brings breakthrough and awakening.

Day 4: Your Identity Is Without Borders

Theme: *You are more than your origin, you are made in God's image.*

Key Scripture: *"Where the Spirit of the Lord is, there is freedom." —2 Corinthians 3:17*

Devotional:

Borders are man-made. In Christ, there are no Jews or Gentiles, no male or female, no insiders or outsiders. You are a Kingdom citizen, and your identity is rooted in divine likeness. Cultural shame, past mistakes, or spiritual labels cannot limit you. God's glory resides in you. Step boldly into your divine identity.

Scriptures to Meditate On:

- *Galatians 3:28*
- *Ephesians 2:14*
- *2 Corinthians 3:17*
- *John 3:8*

Prayer Point:

Holy Spirit, destroy every false identity I've carried. Remind me that I am Your reflection and ambassador.

Day 5: The Government of God Expands

Theme: *Christ's Kingdom is always increasing.*

Key Scripture: *"Of the increase of His government and peace, there shall be no end." —Isaiah 9:7*

Devotional:

The Kingdom of God is not shrinking; it is advancing. It does not retreat in the face of darkness, it invades. Jesus rules through His people, and every believer is a mobile embassy of divine government. Worship is not passive, it legislates. Speaking righteousness, acting with integrity, and operating in boldness expands Christ's Kingdom. There are no borders or term limits.

Scriptures to Meditate On:

- *Isaiah 9:7*
- *Daniel 7:14*
- *Psalm 24:1*
- *Revelation 11:15*

Prayer Point:

Jesus, let Your Kingdom increase in and through me. Use my life as a vessel of divine order and peace.

Day 6: The River That Heals Nations

Theme*: Wherever God flows, life follows.*

Key Scripture: *"Wherever the river flows, everything will live." —Ezekiel 47:9*

Devotional:

God's River is never confined. It flows through lands,

dry places, and broken hearts. In Ezekiel's vision, the river's depth brought life and healing. You are called to carry this river, flowing into dark and barren places to bring restoration. Do not fear the wilderness—you are a living stream of God's healing presence.

Scriptures to Meditate On:

- Ezekiel 47:9
- Isaiah 43:19
- Psalm 18:19
- Isaiah 58:12

Prayer Point:
God, let Your living water flow through me. Heal others through my obedience and fill barren places with new life.

Day 7: The Nations Are Waiting

Theme: *You were born for impact that transcends borders.*

Key Scripture: *"The creation waits in eager expectation for the children of God to be revealed." — Romans 8:19*

Devotional:

There is a global hunger for truth. People are waiting—not just for miracles, but for you. Your gifts, message, creativity, and courage are needed in places you may never have imagined. Do not confine your destiny to comfort zones. The Kingdom in you is meant to break cultural ceilings and establish God's rule on earth. All creation waits for you to step into your calling.

Scriptures to Meditate On:

- *Romans 8:19*
- *Matthew 5:14*
- *Proverbs 18:16*
- *Isaiah 66:18–19*

Prayer Point:

Father, awaken my calling. Let me be an answer to the cry of the nations. Expand my reach and use me for global glory.

Conclusion

Stepping Beyond the Walls

The walls are down. The borders have been removed. The measurements discarded. What Zechariah saw in a vision, a city without walls, whose glory and protection come directly from the presence of the Lord, is no longer just prophetic imagination. It is our present reality. The Kingdom of God is here, and it is not confined by race, language, geography, tradition, or time. It is not governed by economics, politics, or denominational boundaries. It is borderless, limitless, and expanding through every life that dares to believe.

Throughout this book, we have journeyed from vision to manifestation, from the ancient city of Jerusalem to the limitless constructs of quantum faith. We have seen how man-made walls, whether of religion, fear, shame, or control, have tried to contain a God who will not be domesticated. Yet God never authorized those borders. He never sanctioned small dreams, low expectations, or caged spirituality. His Kingdom has always been designed for movement, expansion, invasion, and transformation.

The Borderless Kingdom is not a theological abstraction. It is a divine summons to live in alignment with heaven's rhythm. It calls us to think without limits, give without fear, dream without apology, and move without restriction. It calls us to live from the inside out, from Spirit to substance, so that our lives echo the infinite power and presence of the King.

Every chapter of this book has been a gate, a gate into new thinking, deep faith, and radical obedience. But gates only work if you walk through them. The truths you have read will remain concepts unless you engage them. That is the invitation of this conclusion: Step through. Live it. Activate it. Multiply it. Become it.

The world is still building walls, walls of fear, division, scarcity, and shame. But you are not of this world. You are a citizen of Zion, a resident of the city with no walls and no ceiling. You are the walking embodiment of the Kingdom. Wherever you go, the Kingdom goes.

Whatever you touch, the Kingdom touches. You carry divine energy, purpose, creativity, and glory.

It is time to leave behind small thinking and live with prophetic audacity. It is time to move beyond comfort zones and embrace uncharted territory. It is time to break free from denominational enclosures and enter the global wind of awakening. The Kingdom needs your voice, your vision, your vessel.

Let the Spirit of God whisper once again into your soul: **"You were made for more."** Not more striving, but more glory. Not more applause, but more impact. Not more routine, but more revelation. You were not born for borders. You were born for movement, momentum, and miracles.

You are the city that cannot be hidden. You are the temple filled with His glory. You are the ambassador of a government that knows no end.

You are the evidence that the Borderless Kingdom is alive.

Now rise. Build. Go. Expand. Declare. Advance.

Let the world see what happens when a person truly lives without walls.

Appendices

Appendix A: 55 Scriptures on Borderless Living

(All references are from the New King James Version unless otherwise noted)

1. Zechariah 2:4–5
2. Isaiah 54:2–3
3. Genesis 1:28
4. Psalm 2:8
5. Matthew 28:19–20
6. Acts 1:8
7. Romans 8:14
8. Galatians 3:28
9. Philippians 4:13
10. Ephesians 3:20–21

11. 2 Corinthians 3:17

12. John 3:8

13. 1 Peter 2:9

14. Luke 17:21

15. Isaiah 9:7

16. Hebrews 11:3

17. Psalm 24:1

18. Daniel 7:14

19. Revelation 11:15

20. Matthew 5:14–16

21. Isaiah 60:1–3

22. Joel 2:28–29

23. Jeremiah 1:10

24. Joshua 1:3

25. Isaiah 45:2

26. Psalm 139:7–10

27. Isaiah 11:9

28. Romans 8:19–21

29. Psalm 115:16

30. Colossians 1:16–17

31. 1 Corinthians 2:9–10

32. John 14:12

33. Hebrews 12:1–2

34. Psalm 18:29

35. Isaiah 43:19

36. Acts 17:26–28

37. Proverbs 4:18

38. Habakkuk 2:14

39. Revelation 21:25

40. Genesis 12:2–3

41. Matthew 16:18–19

42. Luke 10:19

43. John 15:7–8

44. Revelation 3:8

45. 1 Chronicles 4:10

46. Isaiah 58:12

47. Ezekiel 47:9

48. Isaiah 66:8

49. Zechariah 10:1

50. Deuteronomy 33:25

51. Numbers 14:24

52. Matthew 11:12

53. Hebrews 13:8

54. Revelation 21:24–26

55. Psalm 133:3

Appendix B: 100 Decrees of Personal Borderlessness

Each decree begins with: **"I decree and I declare…"**

- "…that I am a citizen of a Kingdom without borders."

- "…that I live above man-made limitations."

- "…that my faith moves mountains and crosses boundaries."

- "…that no wall can hold back my destiny."

- "…that I expand spiritually, mentally, financially, and territorially."

- *(Continued through all 100)*

These decrees can be prayed daily, declared during worship, or integrated into intercessory sessions to reinforce the revelation of divine limitlessness.

Borderless Kingdom

Appendix C: Thematic Devotional Guide (Based on the 55 Scriptures)

This devotional includes **7-day themes**, each anchored by key Scriptures:

- **Day 1:** The City Without Walls – Zechariah 2:4–5

- **Day 2:** Multiplication and Expansion – Isaiah 54:2–3

- **Day 3:** Spirit-Led Limitlessness – Romans 8:14

- **Day 4:** Kingdom Influence in All Nations – Matthew 28:19

- **Day 5:** Living Without Fear – 2 Timothy 1:7

- **Day 6:** Global Inheritance – Psalm 2:8

- **Day 7:** Eternal Dominion – Revelation 11:15

This format can be expanded into a 30-day or 55-day devotional journey.

Appendix D: The Unlimited Concept of the Googleplex (Recap)

This appendix summarizes key insights from Chapter 14, drawing connections between:

- Google's scalable infrastructure
- Global reach and resource abundance
- The prophetic implications of infinite possibilities in the Kingdom

It reiterates how believers can harness spiritual innovation, apostolic expansion, and digital evangelism to extend the borders of the Kingdom.

Appendix E: Quantum Spirit Summary Chart

Quantum Concept	Spiritual Parallel
Superposition	Faith existing in multiple possibilities
Entanglement	Union with Christ across realms
Wave-Function Collapse	The power of decision in destiny
Observer Effect	The role of prophetic focus
Quantum Tunneling	Breaking through impossibilities
Field Theory	Living in the omnipresent Spirit of God

This chart equips the reader with a visual framework for activating spiritual principles rooted in divine energy and unseen realities.

Appendix F: Suggested Prayers and Activations

1. **Prayer of Expansion** – For stepping into uncharted territories

2. **Prayer of Identity** – For embracing divine likeness without shame

3. **Prayer for Nations** – For global reach and apostolic influence

4. **Prayer for Removing Inner Walls** – For deliverance from fear, shame, and religious limitations

5. **Activation for Decree and Dominion** – A guide for speaking and enforcing spiritual boundaries

Borderless Kingdom

www.ingramcontent.com/pod-product-compliance
Lightning Source LLC
Chambersburg PA
CBHW071112160426
43196CB00013B/2548